LUXURY HOTELS

AMERICA

edited by Martin Nicholas Kunz, Patrice Farameh & Patricia Massó

teNeues

Chicago

Jackson Hole

Miami Beach

Princess Royal Island

Vancouver

Las Vegas

San Francicso

Boston

Big Sur

New York

Beverly Hills

Honolulu

Paradise Island

Ka'upulehu-Kona

Emerald Bay

Virgin Gorda

Yucatán

Anguilla

St. Martin

Dana Point

St. Barthélemy

Palms Springs

Antigua

Riviera Maya

Puerto Vallarta

St. Lucia

Mustique

Scottsdale

Mexico City

Placencia

São Paulo

San Pedro

Buenos Aires

Luxury Hotels

AMERICA

Extravagance from Canada to Chile

Elite hotels catering to a high-level international clientele now offer more than just a luxurious bed and board away from home. Today, there are new parameters for the label "Luxury Hotel". Aside from impeccable hospitality and creative personalized service that is expected from these five-star resorts, the design and structure must be works of art in pure aesthetics, more spectacular and startling, with an air of theatricality, plunging each guest in the middle of an extravagant arena that combines the comfort of their own home with excitement. But even in the bold way to develop more offbeat, expressive establishments, these hotels are still been composed with familiar images that puts each guest at ease, yet innovative enough to hold the attention of those experienced travelers with a low tolerance for boredom. Resorts such as La Samanna in St. Martin can arrange a private dinner for two on a deserted place on their beach; One&Only Ocean Club in the Bahamas offers a relaxing massage for couples in one of their opulent spa suites; Carlisle Bay in Antigua delivers midnight trays of desserts to a private moonlit terrace overlooking the hushed Caribbean sea. Whether secluded behind the walls of a modernist villa in Chile, or lounging poolside at The Raleigh Hotel in glitzy South Beach, there is always an aura of exclusiveness and a flamboyant stage for the wealthy to enjoy an out-of-ordinary ambience.

Whether set against majestic peaks and lakes of Canada, the lush wood forests and seashores of South America, or the cityscapes of New York and Chicago, these dramatic natural settings influence the appearance and structure of these hotels. The architects have constructed a unique design that complements the varied landscaping, but tempered with comfort and luxury of the resort itself. As society becomes more urbanized, resorts such as the King Pacific Lodge brings each guest close to nature with luxurious suites nestled in the wilderness, as Post Ranch Inn in California capitalizes on its precipitous cliffs, and Le Sereno takes advantage of the shimmering turquoise coral reef cove to create a luxurious refuge protected by ocean waves.

Resort hotels in the Americas have been modeled after Italian villas, Southwestern-style ranches, cabins, tree houses, farmhouses, and even as miniature versions of South Pacific villages. Aside from their unique themed design, these luxury hotels also exaggerate in scale, with generously sized suites that feel very private and residential, but with every possible amenity to set them apart from everyday experience. For instance, few suites can rival those of the legendary private bungalows at the Beverly Hills Hotel, decorated in the purest 1940s style, like little dollhouses, built in the middle of 12 acres of lush gardens with exotic flowers, some with their own swimming pools and gardens, independent entrances, and staff available around the clock.

Even within the bustle of New York City, where buildings have been revamped into sometimes brutally hip and avant-garde structures of design, luxury hotels like The Mercer in Manhattan have comfy loft-like suites that provide silence and relaxation despite its central location. Many of these downtown resorts seem straight from the glossy pages of a designer magazine, with en vogue interiors that scream high style, such as the Mandarin Oriental in New York or the casino-free THEhotel in Las Vegas. Furnishings here are appropriately unobtrusive, since it is the usual designer mantra that the beauty of a place is in its empty spaces.

In the following pages, we present luxury hotels that have become a regular stop on the itinerary of the international jet set today. The resorts are selected by a set of significant common elements; magnificent natural settings in some of the American continent's desirable destinations; faultless hospitality offered by a staff that combines old-world grace and a desire to please each guest; and most importantly, the stunning works of architects and designers that achieve extraordinary and unique spaces.

Patrice Farameh

Extravaganz von Kanada bis Chile

Elite-Hotels mit hochklassiger, internationaler Klientel bieten inzwischen mehr als lediglich die Luxus-Version von Tisch und Bett jenseits der Heimat. Heute bestimmen neue Parameter das Label „Luxus-Hotel". Neben einwandfreier Gastfreundschaft und kreativem, personalisiertem Service, der von diesen Fünf-Sterne-Resorts erwartet wird, müssen Design und Aufmachung Kunstwerken gleichen und Ästhetik pur bieten. Am besten spektakulär und Aufsehen erregend, mit einem Hauch Theatralik, so dass sich jeder Gast wie im Zentrum einer extravaganten Arena fühlt, die den Komfort des eigenen Zuhauses mit besonderer Spannung verbindet. Doch selbst die Hotels, die einen gewagten, unkonventionellen Weg gehen, bieten den gewohnten Service, der jeden Gast zufrieden stellt. Trotzdem sind sie innovativ genug, um die Aufmerksamkeit von erfahrenen Reisenden mit geringer Toleranzschwelle für Langeweile auf sich zu ziehen. Im La Samanna in St. Martin arrangiert man zum Beispiel auf Wunsch ein privates Dinner für Zwei an einer einsamen Stelle des hauseigenen Strandes. Der One&Only Ocean Club auf den Bahamas bietet entspannende Massagen für Paare in einer der opulenten Spa-Suiten. Im Carlisle Bay auf Antigua werden zu Mitternacht Desserts auf einer privaten, mondbeschienenen Terrasse mit Ausblick auf die stille karibische See serviert. Ob hinter den Mauern einer modernen Villa in Chile oder am Pool des The Raleigh Hotels im glitzernden South Beach, die Luxus-Hotels bieten eine Aura von Exklusivität und den Wohlhabenden eine reich dekorierte Bühne, damit sie die ungewöhnliche Atmosphäre genießen können.

Ob vor der Kulisse majestätischer Gipfel und Seen in Kanada, in den üppigen Wäldern und an den Ufern Südamerikas oder in den städtischen Szenerien von New York oder Chicago gelegen, die dramatische Umgebung beeinflusst die Gestaltung dieser Hotels. Die Architekten haben ein einzigartiges Design geschaffen, das sich in die unterschiedlichen Landschaften einfügt, jedoch gemildert wird von Komfort und Luxus. Da die Gesellschaft immer städtischer wird, bringen Resorts wie die King Pacific Lodge mit luxuriösen Suiten, die versteckt in der Wildnis liegen, den Gast zurück zur Natur. Das Post Ranch Inn in Kalifornien nutzt seine steilen Felsen und Le Sereno stellt Dank der schimmernden türkisen Korallenbucht einen luxuriösen Zufluchtsort dar, der von den Wellen des Ozeans geschützt wird.

Die Hotel-Resorts in Amerika wurden nach dem Vorbild italienischer Villen gestaltet, aber auch wie Farmen im Südwesten, wie Kajüten, Baumhäuser, Bauernhäuser und sogar wie Miniaturversionen von südpazifischen Dörfern. Neben ihrem einzigartigen, thematischen Design beeindrucken die Luxus-Hotels durch ihre ausladenden Dimensionen: Die Suiten sind besonders großzügig geschnitten und vermitteln eine private Atmosphäre, die den Gast an Zuhause erinnern soll. Um nicht alltäglich zu wirken, bieten sie allerdings jede denkbare Annehmlichkeit. Nur wenige Suiten können jedoch den legendären privaten Bungalows des Beverly Hills Hotels Konkurrenz machen. Sie liegen in einem knapp fünf Hektar großen, üppigen Garten mit exotischen Blumen und erinnern an kleine Puppenhäuser, eingerichtet ganz im Stil der 1940er Jahre. Einige dieser Häuser haben ihren eigenen Pool, ihren eigenen Garten, einen vom Hotel unabhängigen Eingang sowie Personal, das rund um die Uhr zur Verfügung steht.

Sogar im Gewühl von New York City, wo Gebäude umgestaltet und teilweise in extrem avantgardistische Designstrukturen gepresst wurden, gibt es Luxus-Hotels wie The Mercer in Manhattan. Es hat komfortable Suiten mit Loftcharakter, die trotz ihrer zentralen Lagen Ruhe und Entspannung bieten. Viele dieser innerstädtischen Häuser scheinen direkt den Seiten eines Hochglanz-Designmagazins entsprungen zu sein mit ihren en voguen Einrichtungen von erstklassigem Design. Dazu gehören das Mandarin Oriental in New York und das casinofreie THEhotel in Las Vegas. Ihre Möblierung ist angemessen unaufdringlich, schließlich lautet das Design-Mantra: Die Schönheit des Ortes liegt in seiner Leere.

Auf den folgenden Seiten präsentieren wir Luxus-Hotels, die zu den regelmäßigen Zielen auf der Reiseroute des internationalen Jet-Sets gehören. All diese Anlagen haben einige herausragende Merkmale gemein: Sie liegen in einer atemberaubenden Umgebung an den Traumzielen des amerikanischen Kontinents. Sie bieten tadellose Gastfreundschaft und ein Personal, das den höflichen Service der alten Schule mit dem Willen kombiniert, jeden Gast zufrieden zu stellen. Von größter Bedeutung ist jedoch die herausragende Arbeit von Architekten und Designern, die außergewöhnliche und einzigartige Orte geschaffen haben.

Patrice Farameh

L'extravagance du Canada au Chili

Les hôtels hors du commun fréquentés par une clientèle internationale de grande classe proposent de nos jours autre chose que la version de luxe de la table et du logis loin de chez soi. De nouveaux paramètres définissent désormais le label « Hôtel de luxe ». Outre l'hospitalité irréprochable et le service créatif et personnalisé que l'on attend de ces resorts cinq étoiles, le design et la présentation doivent évoquer des œuvres d'art et incarner une véritable esthétique, frapper de préférence l'imagination et faire sensation, avec une pointe de théâtralisme, de façon que chaque hôte se sente au centre d'une arène extravagante associant le confort de sa propre demeure avec un suspens spécial. Même les hôtels qui optent pour l'audace et le non-conventionnel garantissent le service habituel susceptible de satisfaire tout client. Ils sont cependant assez novateurs pour retenir l'attention des voyageurs expérimentés qui ne supportent quasiment pas de s'ennuyer. Au La Samanna à St. Martin, on organise par exemple sur demande un dîner privé à deux, dans un endroit isolé de la plage privée de l'hôtel. Le One&Only Ocean Club aux Bahamas propose des massages de relaxation pour couples dans l'une de ses opulentes suites spa. Dans le Carlisle Bay à Antigua, des desserts sont servis à minuit sur une terrasse privée, sous un rayon de lune, avec vue sur la mer tranquille des Caraïbes. Que ce soit derrière les murs d'une villa moderne au Chili ou au bord de la piscine du The Raleigh Hotel dans la scintillante South Beach, les hôtels de luxe, entourés d'une aura d'exclusivité, proposent aux clients fortunés une scène richement décorée afin qu'ils puissent profiter pleinement de l'atmosphère insolite.

Qu'ils soient situés devant des sommets et des lacs majestueux au Canada, dans les forêts luxuriantes ou sur les rives de l'Amérique du Sud, ou dans les tissus urbains de New York ou de Chicago, l'environnement impressionnant influence la conception de ces hôtels. Les architectes ont créé un design unique, s'intégrant dans les différents paysages mais atténué par le confort et le luxe. La société s'urbanisant toujours plus, des resorts tels que le King Pacific Lodge avec ses suites luxueuses cachées dans une région déserte, font effectuer à leurs hôtes un retour à la nature. Le Post Ranch Inn en Californie exploite ses rochers abrupts et Le Sereno représente un havre de paix luxueux, grâce à sa baie de corail aux reflets turquoise, protégée des vagues de l'océan.

Les installations hôtelières en Amérique ont été construites sur le modèle des villas italiennes, mais aussi comme des fermes dans le sud-ouest, des cabanes, des maisons en rondins, des fermes et même comme des versions miniatures de villages du Pacifique Sud. Outre leur design thématique exceptionnel, les hôtels de luxe impression-nent par leurs vastes dimensions : les suites sont très généreusement découpées et donnent une impression d'atmosphère privée censée rappeler à l'hôte son bercail. Pour éviter la banalité, elles offrent toutes les commodités imaginables. Mais seules quelques rares suites peuvent rivaliser avec les légendaires bungalows privés du Beverly Hills Hotel. Ils se trouvent dans un parc luxuriant de presque cinq hectares avec des fleurs exotiques et font penser à de petites maisons de poupée, entièrement aménagées dans le style des années 1940. Certains de ces bungalows disposent de leur propre piscine, de leur propre jardin, d'une entrée indépendante de l'hôtel et d'un personnel attitré qui se tient à disposition vingt-quatre heures sur vingt-quatre.

Même dans la cohue de New York City où les bâtiments ont été remodelés et souvent accolés dans des structures conceptuelles avant-gardistes, il y a des hôtels de luxe comme The Mercer à Manhattan. Malgré son emplacement très central, il possède des suites proches du loft où règnent calme et détente. Nombre de ces établissements de centre ville semblent sortir tout droit des pages glacées d'un magazine de design, avec leurs aménagements en vogue d'une conception très classe. Parmi eux, le Mandarin Oriental à New York et THEhotel sans casino à Las Vegas. Leur ameublement témoigne d'une discrétion de bon ton, le credo du design étant que la beauté du lieu réside dans sa vacuité.

Les pages qui suivent vous présentent des hôtels de luxe visités régulièrement par la jet-set internationale en voyage. Tous ces établissements partagent quelques caractéri-stiques exceptionnelles : ils se trouvent dans des environnements à couper le souffle, dans les endroits de rêve du continent américain. Ils offrent une hospitalité parfaite et un personnel qui allie la politesse du service de l'ancienne école au désir de satisfaire chaque client. Le plus important toutefois est le travail extraordinaire des architectes et des designers qui ont su créer des lieux uniques et hors du commun.

Patrice Farameh

Extravagancia de Canadá a Chile

Los hoteles de élite que acogen a la exclusiva clientela internacional han dejado de ser simplemente una versión de lujo del hecho de comer y dormir fuera de casa. Hoy existen nuevos parámetros que definen la etiqueta de "hotel de lujo". Al margen de la intachable hospitalidad y el servicio personalizado y creativo que se da por hecho en estos resorts de cinco estrellas, ahora la presentación y el diseño deben alcanzar niveles artísticos y la más pura estética. Y a ser posible, de forma espectacular y llamativa, con un toque de teatralidad que haga sentir al huésped en el centro de un escenario de extravagancia, en el que el confort de casa se convierte en una experiencia excitante. Pero incluso los hoteles que siguen una línea atrevida y fuera de lo convencional, ofrecen también un servicio habitual capaz de satisfacer a todo tipo de cliente. Si bien siempre son lo suficientemente innovadores como para atraer la atención de aquéllos que están habituados a viajar y toleran poco la falta de originalidad. En La Samanna, St. Martin, por ejemplo, se puede disponer una cena privada para dos en un rincón solitario de la playa del hotel a petición del cliente. El One&Only Ocean Club en Bahamas ofrece masajes relajantes para parejas en cualquiera de sus opulentas suites spa. En Carlisle Bay, Antigua, se sirve el postre a medianoche en una terraza privada a la luz de la luna y con el sosegado mar Caribe como espectáculo. Ya sea tras los muros de una moderna villa en Chile, o en la piscina del The Raleigh Hotel en la glamorosa South Beach, los hoteles de lujo se envuelven de un aura de exclusividad y crean un escenario suntuoso en el que los más acomodados puedan gozar de un ambiente fuera de lo común.

Si hay algo que determine claramente la configuración de estos hoteles es el arrebatador entorno en el que están ubicados; ya se trate de un espectacular escenario con las majestuosas cumbres y lagos de Canadá, las exuberantes selvas y costas de Suramérica, o la escena urbana de Nueva York o Chicago. Los arquitectos han concebido un diseño excepcional que se funde en los diversos paisajes y se ve suavizado con confort y lujo. En un momento en el que la sociedad cada vez se hace más urbana, resorts como el King Pacific Lodge con sus lujosas suites escondidas en un paisaje salvaje, devuelven al huésped el contacto con la naturaleza. Mientras que el Post Ranch Inn en California aprovecha sus rocas escarpadas, Le Sereno se convierte en refugio de lujo gracias a una bahía de coral de un resplandeciente turquesa, protegida de las olas del océano.

Los Hotel Resorts en América han sido diseñados siguiendo los modelos de villas italianas, granjas del suroeste, casas sobre árboles, camarotes, casas campesinas e incluso versiones miniatura de pequeños pueblos del Pacífico Sur. A los excepcionales diseños temáticos se unen las bastas dimensiones que ocupan estos hoteles de lujo. Las suites están dotadas de gran amplitud y transmiten al huésped un ambiente de privacidad con ánimo de que todo ello le recuerde a estar como en casa. Y, a la vez, para no dar la sensación de rutina, le ofrecen todo tipo de comodidades imaginables. Sólo unas pocas suites pueden competir con los legendarios bungalows del Beverly Hills Hotel, que aparecen como casitas de muñecas, diseñadas en estilo de la década de 1940 e insertadas en un frondoso jardín de apenas cinco hectáreas, cuajado de flores exóticas. Algunas de ellas cuentan con piscina y jardín propios, entrada independiente del hotel y un personal a plena disposición las veinticuatro horas del día.

Incluso inmersos en la agitación de New York City, donde los edificios se transforman y se comprimen creando a veces estructuras de diseño extremadamente vanguardistas, existen hoteles de lujo como The Mercer en Manhattan. Éste alberga confortables suites estilo loft, que a pesar de su ubicación céntrica ofrecen relax y silencio. Muchos de estos hoteles urbanos parecen sacados de la portada de revistas de diseño glamoroso, con su decoración de moda y exquisitos diseños de primera línea. Entre ellos se encuentran el Mandarin Oriental de Nueva York y el hotel sin casino THEhotel en Las Vegas. Su mobiliario es apropiado y sereno, puesto que, como reza el mantra del diseño, "la belleza del lugar reside en su vacío".

En estas páginas se presentan hoteles de lujo que se incluyen en los destinos de viaje habituales de la Jet set. En todos ellos resalta una característica común: la ubicación dentro de un entorno espectacular en los lugares de ensueño del continente americano. Todos ofrecen una hospitalidad intachable y disponen de un personal que combina la amabilidad de la vieja escuela y el deseo de satisfacer a cada cliente. Si bien es cierto que lo más importante es el trabajo sobresaliente de los arquitectos y diseñadores que han concebido estos lugares excepcionales y únicos.

Patrice Farameh

Stravaganza del Canada al Cile

Gli hotel esclusivi che possono vantarsi di una clientela scelta ed internazionale ormai promettono molto di più di un ristorante e di una camera di lusso in un luogo che non sia la propria casa. Oggi, il concetto di "hotel di lusso" è definito da nuovi parametri: oltre alla perfetta ospitalità e al servizio creativo e personalizzato che ci si attende in questi resort a cinque stelle, occorre che il design e lo stile siano capolavori esteticamente ineccepibili. Nel migliore dei casi, essi devono suscitare ammirazione e stupore al tempo stesso, e non essere privi di un tocco di teatralità: Così, l'ospite si sente al centro di una straordinaria arena, in cui il comfort della propria casa si colora di una particolare eccitazione. Anche gli hotel di tipo non convenzionale offrono il consueto servizio, in grado di soddisfare ogni cliente; allo stesso tempo, però, essi sono abbastanza innovativi da attirare l'attenzione di viaggiatori esperti con una bassa soglia di tolleranza per la noia. Al La Samanna di St. Martin, ad esempio, è possibile organizzare, su richiesta, una cena privata per due in un angolo appartato della spiaggia dell'hotel. L'One&Only Ocean Club, alle Bahamas, propone rilassanti massaggi per coppie in una delle sofisticate suite della Spa. Ad Antigua, al Carlisle Bay, a mezzanotte si servono dessert al chiaro di luna su una terrazza privata con vista sul calmo e silenzioso Mar dei Caraibi. Sia dietro le mura di una moderna villa in Cile, sia intorno alla piscina del The Raleigh Hotel sulla scintillante South Beach, gli hotel di lusso offrono agli ospiti benestanti un tocco di esclusività ed una colorata scenografia in cui godere di questa straordinaria atmosfera.

Poco importa se lo scenario è costituito dalle vette maestose e i laghi del Canada, dalle lussureggianti foreste sulle coste del Sudamerica o piuttosto da città come New York o Chicago: il favoloso paesaggio influenza lo stile di questi hotel. Gli architetti hanno realizzato un design, unico nel suo genere, che s'inserisce perfettamente nei diversi contesti e a cui comfort e lusso danno il tocco finale. Poiché la società diventa sempre più cittadina, un resort come il King Pacific Lodge, con le sue lussuose suite nascoste nel paesaggio selvaggio, riporta l'ospite alla natura. Il Post Ranch Inn, in California, valorizza le sue scogliere scoscese ed il Le Sereno, con la baia corallina dai riflessi turchesi, è un ritiro lussuoso al riparo dalle onde dell'oceano.

I resort americani sono stati realizzati nello stile delle ville italiane, ma anche come fattorie del Sud-ovest, cabine di navi, capanne su alberi, casolari e addirittura come versioni in miniatura di villaggi del Pacifico. Accanto al design, unico nel loro genere, gli hotel di lusso incantano per la loro spaziosità: le suite, particolarmente ampie, ispirano un'atmosfera di privato che fa sentire gli ospiti a casa loro e, ben lungi dall'essere ordinarie, offrono ogni sorta di comfort. Solo poche suite riescono tuttavia a fare concorrenza ai leggendari bungalow privati del Beverly Hills Hotel: situate in un lussureggiante giardino di circa cinque ettari, circondate da fiori esotici, ricordano piccole case di bambola e sono completamente arredate nello stile degli anni 1940. Alcune di esse dispongono di una piscina e di un giardino proprio, di un'entrata indipendente e di personale disponibile ventiquattro ore su ventiquattro.

Addirittura nella confusione di New York City, dove tanti edifici sono stati completamente ristrutturati e, talvolta, compressi in strutture di design d'avanguardia, esistono degli hotel di lusso come The Mercer di Manhattan. Le sue suite confortevoli, simili a un loft, offrono tranquillità e relax nonostante la posizione centrale. Molti di questi edifici cittadini, con i loro arredamenti en vogue di stile eccezionale, sembrano usciti direttamente dalle pagine patinate delle riviste di design. Il Mandarin Oriental di New York e il THEhotel di Las Vegas, privo di sala da gioco, ne sono un esempio: l'arredamento è opportunamente sobrio, all'insegna della regola che vuole che siano gli spazi vuoti a rendere bello un luogo.

Le seguenti pagine presentano alcuni hotel di lusso che sono meta abituale del jet-set internazionale. Tutti hanno in comune delle caratteristiche fondamentali: sono situati in un paesaggio mozzafiato nei luoghi più belli del continente americano ed abbinano la perfetta ospitalità al servizio di un personale che unisce una cortesia ineccepibile al proposito di soddisfare le esigenze di ogni ospite. La cosa più importante, tuttavia, è lo straordinario lavoro degli architetti e dei designer che hanno realizzato questi luoghi unici ed eccezionali.

Patrice Farameh

King Pacific Lodge
A Rosewood Resort

Princess Royal Island, British Columbia, Canada

If luxury hotels were judged on location alone, King Pacific Lodge would be up there with the best. Situated amidst pristine nature, this exclusive retreat is one of the furthest north on Canada's Pacific coast. Guests can look forward to a grandiose wooden lodge with a select number of rustically styled rooms. What it lacks in quantity, it more than makes up for in quality—spacious and comfortable with luxurious bathrooms, each room directly overlooks the ocean or surrounding woodland.

Wenn derart unberührte Natur bereits Luxus darstellte, dann wäre die King Pacific Lodge allein aufgrund ihrer Umgebung exklusiv. Doch der abgelegene, fast nördlichste Zufluchtsort der kanadischen Pazifikküste beschränkt sich nicht nur auf diesen Vorzug. Der palastartige Holzbau bietet wenige, dafür aber großzügige Gästezimmer. Ihr Stil: Rustikal und von hohem Komfort, was sich vor allem an den herrschaftlichen Bädern zeigt. Jeder Raum erlaubt einen direkten Blick auf das Meer oder die umliegenden Wälder.

Si l'on considère que la nature intacte est un grand luxe, le King Pacific Lodge est par conséquent un complexe exclusif de par son environnement. Mais ce lieu de refuge isolé, situé quasiment au point le plus au nord de la côte pacifique canadienne, ne présente pas que cet avantage. Semblable à un palais, le bâtiment en bois compte peu de chambres, mais elles sont généreuses. Leur style : rustique et de grand confort, comme le montrent principalement les salles de bain princières. On bénéficie dans chaque pièce d'une vue directe sur la mer ou sur les forêts environnantes.

Ya sólo por el lujo que representa la naturaleza salvaje de su entorno, el King Pacific Lodge es un lugar exclusivo. Pero este apartado refugio, casi el más septentrional de la costa pacífica canadiense, no se reduce a semejante privilegio. La construcción en madera con aire palaciego ofrece pocas, pero amplias habitaciones para huéspedes. El estilo es rústico y dotado de gran confort; muestra de ello son sus señoriales cuartos de baño. Las habitaciones ofrecen vistas directas al mar o a los bosques aledaños.

Se la natura incontaminata rappresentasse di per sé il lusso, allora il King Pacific Lodge si potrebbe considerare esclusivo già solo per la sua ubicazione. Ma essa non costituisce l'unico vantaggio di questo luogo isolato, quasi il più settentrionale della costa canadese del Pacifico. La sontuosa costruzione in legno dispone di poche ma spaziose camere. Lo stile: rustico ma dotato di tutti i comfort, come dimostrano soprattutto i bagni signorili. Tutte le stanze godono di vista sull'oceano o sui boschi circostanti.

Bathed in a twilight glow: King Pacific Lodge. In the warm season from May to October the hotel offers exclusive wilderness packages.

Im Glanz der tiefen Sonne: King Pacific Lodge. In den warmen Monaten von Mai bis Oktober bietet das Haus exklusiven Natururlaub.

Dans les rayons du soleil bas : le King Pacific Lodge. L'hôtel propose de passer des vacances exclusives dans la nature au cours des mois chauds, de mai à octobre.

En el esplendor del sol profundo: King Pacific Lodge. En los meses cálidos de mayo a octubre, la casa propone vacaciones exclusivas en medio de la naturaleza.

Nella scia del sole all'orizzonte: King Pacific Lodge. Il lodge offre vacanze esclusive all'insegna della natura nei caldi mesi compresi fra maggio ed ottobre.

The wooden styling of the lodge sits in perfect harmony with the idyllic setting, emphasizing the vivid impression of "getting back to nature".

Die traumhafte Lage wird durch den besonderen Charme des Hauses ergänzt und macht die King Pacific Lodge zu einem wahren Erholungsparadies. Durch den großzügigen Einsatz von Hölzern wird die Naturverbundenheit unterstrichen.

L'emplacement de rêve est complété par le charme particulier de l'hôtel et fait du King Pacific Lodge un véritable paradis de détente. L'utilisation généreuse de différents types de bois permet de souligner le lien avec la nature.

Su ubicación de ensueño armoniza con el encanto de la casa, lo que hace del King Pacific Lodge un verdadero paraíso de descanso. El empleo de la madera en la decoración acentúa sus vínculos con la naturaleza.

L'ubicazione quasi irreale trova continuazione nel fascino tutto particolare della struttura, così facendo del King Pacific Lodge un vero e proprio angolo di paradiso ideale per il relax. L'ampio utlizzo di diverse varietà di legno all'interno sottolinea l'idea di totale immersione nella natura.

King Pacific Lodge, A Rosewood Resort *Princess Royal Island, British Columbia, Canada*   17

Opus
Vancouver, British Columbia, Canada

Where even the concierge is kitted out with a trendy outfit. Contemporary design is the order of the day in this chic hotel with its well-defined modern styling. Though minimalist in decor, the rooms, suites and studios boast vibrant colors and high-quality furnishings. Translucent walls let plenty of light into the spacious bathrooms, which offer all kinds of fancy frills and luxuries. A unique blend of styles characterize the Opus Bar, while the hotel brasserie adds a touch of *belle époque* flair.

Schon die Concierge empfängt im trendbewussten Outfit. Hier herrscht durchgängig zeitgemäßer Stil. Der Schick des Hauses ist klar und klassisch modern. Die Räume, Suiten und Studios zeigen sich reduziert im Dekor, dafür kräftig in den Farben und anspruchsvoll in der Ausstattung. Die Badezimmer sind groß, transparent und bieten diverse Annehmlichkeiten. Von ganz eigenem Design-Mix ist die Opus Bar, die Brasserie des Hauses verströmt dazu einen Hauch von Flair der Belle Époque.

C'est vêtue d'une tenue à la mode que la concierge accueille les visiteurs. Le style contemporain règne ici avec constance. Le style de la maison est épuré ainsi que moderne et classique à la fois. Les pièces, les suites et les studios présentent un décor minimaliste, mais les couleurs sont vives et l'équipement est recherché. Les salles de bain sont grandes, transparentes et offrent diverses commodités. Le bar Opus est caractérisé par un mélange de design propre à l'hôtel, la brasserie de l'hôtel dégage un charme digne de la Belle Époque.

Un portero con atuendo moderno recibe a los huéspedes. Aquí domina siempre un estilo contemporáneo. El estilo chic de la casa se basa en el modernismo clásico. Las habitaciones, suites y estudios destacan por su decoración austera, que sin embargo crea contraste gracias a sus colores fuertes y un mobiliario exclusivo. Los cuartos de baño son grandes, luminosos y ofrecen diversas comodidades. El bar Opus muestra una genuina fusión de diseño; de la cervecería de la casa emana un toque Belle Époque.

Già uno sguardo alla concierge basta per capire che la veste in cui si presenta l'hotel è chic contemporanea. Lo stile che lo contraddistingue è sobrio e classico-moderno. Le stanze, le suite e gli appartamenti denotano una propensione ad una voluta riduzione degli elementi decorativi, compensata da una scelta decisa nelle tonalità cromatiche e da un arredamento ricercato. I bagni sono ampi, dotati di vetrate a tutta altezza nonché di diversi comfort. Una peculiare mescolanza di stili è il tocco distintivo del Opus Bar, mentre la brasserie emana un fascino vagamente belle époque.

The Opus Hotel is situated in Vancouver's Yaletown district, where movies stars and design connoisseurs love to hang out.

Im Yaletown-District von Vancouver liegt das Hotel Opus: geschätzt von Filmstars und begehrt bei Design-Liebhabern.

L'hôtel Opus est situé dans le district Yaletown de Vancouver, apprécié des stars du cinéma et recherché par les amoureux du design.

En el Yaletown District de Vancouver se ubica el Hotel Opus apreciado por estrellas de cine y codiciado por los amantes del diseño.

Ubicato nel distretto Yaletown di Vancouver, l'Opus Hotel è apprezzato dai personaggi più "in" del mondo del cinema e dagli appassionati di design.

Whether it's the penthouse studio, deluxe suite or a standard room, vibrant colors and well-defined shapes dominate throughout.

Ob Penthouse-Studio, Deluxe-Suite oder Standardzimmer — im Opus dominieren kräftige Farben und klare Formen.

Qu'il s'agisse d'un studio mansardé, d'une suite Deluxe ou d'une chambre standard, les couleurs vives et les formes claires sont dominantes dans l'hôtel Opus.

Ya sea en el "penthouse studio", la suite Deluxe o una habitación estándar —en Opus dominan los colores intensos y las formas bien definidas.

Poco importa se penthouse studio, suite deluxe o camera standard: all'Opus predominano tonalità cromatiche decise e linee ben definite.

Four Seasons Resort Hualalai

Ka'upulehu-Kona, Hawaii

Along the exclusive Kona-Kohala coastline, dazzling white sandy beaches contrast with black volcanic rock. These lava deposits are responsible for giving Hawaii's Pacific waters the deep azure color that is almost unique to the island. Set amidst lush vegetation, the resort's 36 lodges house 243 rooms and suites, all exquisitely furnished in a traditional Hawaiian style. There is also a private golf course designed by Jack Nicklaus, which offers spectacular views of the ocean.

An der exklusiven Kona-Kohala-Küste treffen blendend weiße Sandstrände auf schwarzes Lavagestein, das dem Wasser des Pazifiks die tiefblaue Färbung gibt, wie sie fast nur um Hawaii zu finden ist. Die 36 Bungalows des Resorts sind eingebettet in üppig grüne Vegetation. Sie beherbergen 243 Gästezimmer und Suiten, die im landestypischen Stil exklusiv eingerichtet wurden. Spektakuläre Ausblicke auf den Ozean bietet der von Jack Nicklaus entworfene Golfplatz.

Sur la côte exclusive de Kona-Kohala, des plages de sable blanc immaculé côtoient des pierres de lave noire qui donnent à l'eau du Pacifique cette couleur bleu marine que l'on ne trouve presque qu'à Hawaï. Les 36 bungalows du complexe se fondent dans une végétation verte luxuriante. Ils hébergent 243 chambres et suites qui ont été exclusivement aménagées conformément au style typique du pays. Le terrain de golf conçu par Jack Nicklaus garantit des points de vue spectaculaires sur l'océan.

En la exclusiva costa Kona-Kohala se fusionan a la perfección las playas blancas y la negra roca volcánica que otorga al pacífico su profundo color azul; un fenómeno casi exclusivo de Hawai. Los 36 bungalows del resort están integrados en medio de una exuberante vegetación y disponen de 243 exclusivas habitaciones y suites decoradas en el estilo típico de la isla. El campo de golf diseñado por Jack Nicklaus ofrece una vista espectacular al océano.

Lungo l'esclusiva costa di Kona-Kohala, le spiagge bianchissime orlano la nera pietra vulcanica, la stessa che dona all'acqua del Pacifico quella tonalità blu intenso che lambisce quasi esclusivamente le Hawaii. Immersi nella vegetazione verde intenso, i 36 bungalow del resort alloggiano le 243 camere degli ospiti e suite raffinatamente arredate in tipico stile locale. Dal campo da golf firmato Jack Nicklaus si gode una splendida vista sull'oceano.

The resort is set in a huge two-mile-long bay in the north-west of the island.

Gut zwei Kilometer lang ist die Bucht im Nordwesten der Insel, an der das Resort liegt.

Au nord-ouest de l'île, la baie sur laquelle se trouve le complexe fait deux kilomètres de long.

La bahía de la parte noroeste de la isla en la que está ubicado el resort recorre más de dos kilómetros.

La baia che lambisce il resort a nordovest dell'isola si estende per ben due chilometri.

Dark-colored woods and vibrant tones lend the rooms a typical Hawaiian charm. The hotel spa offers traditional treatments such as the four-handed Lomi Lomi massage.

Dunkle Hölzer und kräftige Farben geben den Zimmern ihre typisch hawaiische Anmutung. Im Spa werden traditionelle Behandlungen wie die vierhändige Lomi-Lomi-Massage angeboten.

Bois sombres et couleurs vives confèrent aux chambres leur charme hawaïen typique. Des soins traditionnels comme le massage « Lomi Lomi » à quatre mains sont dispensés dans le spa.

Maderas oscuras y colores vivos le confieren a las habitaciones su típico ambiente hawaiano. En el spa se ofrecen tratamientos tradicionales como el masaje lomi lomi a cuatro manos.

Legni scuri e colori decisi conferiscono alle stanze un'atmosfera tipicamente hawaiana. Oltre ai tradizionali trattamenti corpo, la Spa propone anche il massaggio "Lomi Lomi" a quattro mani.

Sheraton Moana Surfrider

Honolulu, Haiwaii

Alongside its evocative architecture, the Sheraton Moana Surfrider has all the luxury facilities and excellent service you'd expect from a contemporary top-class hotel. Situated right by the Pacific waters in Hawaii's capital city, the hotel is steeped in over 100 years of history. These historic surroundings provide the perfect setting for a dream wedding—whether on the roof terrace with its panoramic views of the ocean, on the white sandy beach or in the hotel garden.

Das nostalgische Erscheinungsbild des Sheraton Moana Surfrider bildet zusammen mit den Annehmlichkeiten und dem Service der heutigen Zeit eine perfekte Symbiose. Direkt am pazifischen Ozean in der Hauptstadt Hawaiis gelegen, blickt das Hotel auf eine über 100-jährige Geschichte zurück. In diesem historischen Ambiente können Traumhochzeiten gefeiert werden, ob nun auf der Dachterrasse mit weitem Blick über das Meer, am weißen Strand oder im Garten.

L'apparence nostalgique du Sheraton Moana Surfrider ainsi que le service et les commodités modernes créent une ensemble parfaite. Situé au bord de l'océan Pacifique dans la capitale de Hawaï, l'hôtel a une histoire de 100 ans. Cette ambiance historique est l'idéal pour fêter des mariages de rêve, que ce soit sur la terrasse du toit avec une large vue sur la mer, sur la plage de sable blanc ou dans le jardin.

La imagen nostálgica del Sheraton Moana Surfrider forma una simbiosis perfecta con las comodidades y el servicio de hoy. Este hotel situado frente al océano pacífico, en la capital de Hawai, cuenta con más de 100 años de historia. En este ambiente histórico se celebran bodas de ensueño, ya sea en la terraza con vistas al mar, en las blancas playas o en el jardín.

Il fascino nostalgico dello Sheraton Moana Surfrider unito ai comfort e al servizio in grado di soddisfare le esigenze più attuali creano una perfetta simbiosi. Situato direttamente sulla spiaggia orlata dall'Oceano Pacifico nella capitale delle Hawaii, l'hotel vanta una storia di oltre 100 anni. Il contesto ideale per festeggiare un matrimonio da favola, a scelta sulla terrazza sul tetto con ampia vista sull'oceano, sulla spiaggia candida o in giardino.

The breakfast terrace is the perfect place to start your day.

Die Frühstücksterrasse lädt zum Verweilen ein.

La terrasse prévue pour les petits déjeuners invite au repos.

La terraza para desayunos invita a dejar pasar el tiempo.

La terrazza per colazioni invita a fermarsi per una breve sosta mattutina.

Many of the suites offer picturesque views of Waikiki beach.

Viele der Suiten bieten einen traumhaften Blick auf den Waikiki Beach.

De nombreuses suites offrent une vue de rêve sur la Waikiki Beach.

Muchas de las suites ofrecen una vista maravillosa a Waikiki Beach.

Da molte delle suite si gode una fantastica vista sulla Waikiki Beach.

Amangani

Jackson Hole, Wyoming

Wyoming's wild landscape is home to Asia-based Aman Group's first luxury hotel in the U.S. The grounds are centered around an elongated building whose hip roof mimics the contours of the rocky scenery. Covered with cedar wood slates, it could almost be a mountain ledge. The exquisitely decorated interior nods to the simpler life associated with log cabins—polished wooden slats conceal soft lighting, while perfectly sculpted tree stumps serve as tables.

In der wilden Landschaft Wyomings hat die asiatische Aman-Gruppe ihr erstes Haus in den USA platziert. Das langgestreckte Gebäude fügt sich in das Gelände ein, sein Walmdach nimmt die Umrisse der charakteristischen Felsenlandschaft auf. Eingedeckt mit Zedernholzschindeln wirkt es fast wie ein Felsvorsprung. Die Interieurs sind edel und doch erlauben sie die Assoziation eines einfachen Lebens in einer Blockhütte: Indirektes Licht verbirgt sich hinter plan geschliffenen Brettern, als Tisch fungiert ein perfekt bearbeiteter Baumstumpf.

C'est dans le paysage sauvage du Wyoming que le groupe asiatique Aman a installé son premier hôtel aux États-Unis. Le bâtiment allongé se fond dans le terrain, son toit en croupe épouse les contours du paysage rocheux caractéristique. Couvert de bardeaux en cèdre, il ressemble presque à une corniche. Les intérieurs sont élégants, mais ils permettent cependant d'y associer un mode de vie simple dans une cabane en rondins : la lumière indirecte est cachée derrière des planches surfacées, et une souche d'arbre parfaitement travaillé sert de table.

El grupo asiático Aman ha elegido este paisaje salvaje de Wyoming para ubicar su primer hotel en los Estados Unidos. El largo edificio se integra en el paisaje y su tejado a cuatro aguas toma la silueta del característico paisaje rocoso. El techo cubierto con ripia de madera de cedro simula un saliente de roca. El interior, aunque elegante, transmite la sencillez de una cabaña de madera: La luz indirecta se oculta detrás de pantallas de madera, un tronco de árbol de perfecto acabado hace de mesa.

È nel paesaggio selvaggio dello Wyoming che il gruppo asiatico Aman ha collocato il suo primo resort costruito negli Stati Uniti. La struttura oblunga, come incastonata nel paesaggio roccioso e sovrastata da un tetto a padiglione, si armonizza perfettamente con l'ambiente circostante: rivestito di scandole di cedro, sembra scaturire dalla montagna come uno sperone roccioso. Gli arredamenti interni sono ricercati e nel contempo consoni all'ideale di una vita semplice ispirato dalla struttura in legno. La luce indiretta si nasconde dietro assi levigate, dei ceppi perfettamente lavorati fungono da tavolo.

Oklahoma sandstone and lovingly finished wood conjure up an atmosphere of elegant simplicity.

Sandstein aus Oklahoma und sorgfältig bearbeitetes Holz kreieren einen Stil edler Schlichtheit.

Le grès d'Oklahoma et le bois travaillé avec soin créent un style simple et élégant.

La arenisca de Oklahoma y maderas perfectamente trabajadas crean un estilo de elegante sencillez.

Pietra arenaria dell'Oklahoma e legno lavorato con cura contribuiscono a creare uno stile di raffinata semplicità.

The hotel pool offers a stupendous view of the Rocky Mountains and the Snake River. All 40 suites boast an open fireplace made from patinized metal.

Vom Pool aus eröffnet sich ein grandioser Blick auf die Gipfel der Rocky Mountains und den Snake River. Jede der 40 Suiten besitzt einen offenen Kamin aus patiniertem Metall.

La piscine offre une vue grandiose sur les sommets des Rocky Mountains et le Snake River. Les 40 suites possèdent chacune une cheminée ouverte en métal patiné.

Desde la piscina se aprecia una grandiosa vista de la cima de las Montañas Rocosas y del río Snaker. Cada una de las 40 suites posee una chimenea de metal envejecido.

Sensazionale il panorama sulle vette delle Montagne Rocciose e sullo Snake River. Tutte le 40 suite sono dotate di camino aperto in metallo patinato.

Four Seasons Hotel San Francisco

San Francisco, California

Luxurious hotel towers over the Financial District of San Francisco, sandwiched between multimillion-dollar condos and elite shops. Spacious rooms are decorated in soothing hues of green, beige, and taupe, with custom-made bedding, original contemporary artwork, and huge luxury marble bathrooms. The 277 guest rooms include 46 suites with floor-to-ceiling windows overlooking the bay, or stunning views of the city.

Das luxuriöse Hotel erhebt sich über den Finanzdistrikt von San Francisco. Es ist umgeben von Eigentumswohnungen im Wert mehrerer Millionen Dollar und exklusiven Geschäften. Die 277 geräumigen Zimmer sind in beruhigenden Grün-, Beige- und Grauschattierungen gehalten. Zum Standard gehören maßgefertigte Betten, zeitgenössische Kunst und ein riesiges, luxuriöses Marmorbad. In den 46 Suiten des Hotels reichen die Fenster vom Boden bis zur Decke. Von dort hat der Gast einen atemberaubenden Blick auf die Bucht und die Stadt.

Cet hôtel de luxe surplombe le quartier financier de San Francisco. Il est entouré d'appartements à plusieurs millions de dollars et de magasins exclusifs. Dans les 277 chambres spacieuses, des dégradés de couleurs apaisantes comme le vert, beige et gris dominent. L'aménagement standard comprend des lits fabriqués sur mesure, des œuvres d'art contemporain et une immense salle de bain luxueuse en marbre. Dans les 46 suites de l'hôtel, les fenêtres occupent toute la hauteur des pièces. L'hôte jouit ainsi d'une vue époustouflante sur la baie et la ville.

Este fastuoso hotel se eleva sobre el distrito financiero de San Francisco, rodeado de comercios exclusivos y viviendas valoradas en varios millones de dólares. Sus 277 habitaciones de gran amplitud se muestran en suaves tonos verdes, beiges y grises. De su oferta estándar forman parte camas hechas a medida, arte contemporáneo, así como un extenso y lujoso cuarto de baño de mármol. Los ventanales de las 46 suites se extienden desde el suelo al techo. Justo desde aquí los huéspedes pueden disfrutar de una vista fantástica sobre la bahía y la ciudad.

Questo lussuoso hotel, situato al di sopra del distretto finanziario di San Francisco, è circondato da appartamenti da decine di milioni di dollari e da negozi esclusivi. I tenui toni del verde, del beige e tutte le sfumature del grigio sono i colori che prevalgono nell'arredamento delle 277 spaziose camere. Il servizio standard comprende letti confezionati su misura, oggetti d'arte contemporanea ed un grandissimo e lussuoso bagno di marmo. Nelle 46 suite, finestre extradimensionate si allungano dal pavimento al soffitto, regalando agli ospiti una vista mozzafiato sulla baia e sulla città.

15,000 square-feet of flexible indoor / outdoor space is available for special events and business meetings, offering views of the city skyline.

Rund 1400 Quadratmeter mit Blick auf die Skyline stehen innen und außen für private und geschäftliche Veranstaltungen zur Verfügung.

Quelque 1400 mètres carrés avec vue sur la silhouette urbaine sont à votre disposition pour des réceptions privées et professionnelles.

Alrededor de 1400 metros cuadrados con vistas al contorno de la ciudad están disponibles para la celebración de eventos privados o de negocios, tanto en espacios interiores como exteriores.

All'interno ed all'esterno del complesso sono disponibili circa 1400 metri quadrati di superficie con vista sullo skyline per manifestazioni private e di lavoro.

42 stories towering over the heart of downtown; a perfect combination of elegance and modern luxury with a vibe that combines sophistication with trendy.

42 Stockwerke ragen im Herzen des Zentrums empor; eine perfekte Kombination von Eleganz und modernem Luxus, gehoben und trendig zugleich.

42 étages se dressent au cœur du centre ville ; la parfaite combinaison de l'élégance et du luxe moderne, à la fois exclusif et à la mode.

42 plantas se alzan en pleno corazón de la ciudad; una perfecta combinación de elegancia y moderno lujo que denota exclusividad y marca la tendencia.

Un edificio di 42 piani si innalza nel cuore del centro: eleganza e lusso moderno si incontrano creando un insieme esclusivo e trendy al tempo stesso.

Post Ranch Inn

Big Sur, California

Set 1,200 feet above the sea is California's secret laid-back luxury resort that is both modern and rustic, as well as environmentally aware. Stylish accommodations consist mainly of perched up on the cliff, with a cozy fireplace, marble Jacuzzi spa tub, and a private deck with wide-angle mountain and ocean views. Amenities include in-room spa treatments, meditative yoga in a circular canvas yurt, as well as lectures on stargazing.

Rund 365 Meter über dem Meer liegt dieser kalifornische Geheimtipp. Ein entspanntes und doch sehr luxuriöses Resort mit umweltbewusster Haltung. Die separaten Häuser liegen Hügel aufwärts am Fels und verbinden moderne mit rustikalen Elementen. Jedes Haus hat einen Kamin, einen Marmorwhirlpool und eine Terrasse mit Panoramablick auf die Berge oder den Ozean. Zum außergewöhnlichen Angebot gehören Spa-Behandlungen auf dem Zimmer, meditatives Yoga in einer runden Leinen-Jurte sowie astrologische Vorträge.

A quelque 365 mètres au-dessus de la mer se trouve cet endroit confidentiel en Californie. Une villégiature à l'ambiance détendue, très luxueuse mais aussi respectueuse de l'environnement. Les villas séparées grimpent la colline, accrochées au rocher. Associant éléments modernes et rustiques, chacune possède sa cheminée, ses bains bouillonnants en marbre et sa terrasse avec vue panoramique sur les montagnes ou l'océan. Les prestations exceptionnelles proposent des soins spa en chambre, du yoga méditatif dans une yourte ronde en toile ainsi que des conférences sur l'astronomie.

Aproximadamente a 365 metros sobre el mar se encuentra ubicado este escondite californiano. Un resort relajante y lujoso en respetuosa fusión con el medio ambiente. En las casas separadas, situadas en las rocas colina arriba se combinan elementos modernos y rústicos. Cada una de ellas cuenta con una chimenea, un jacuzzi de mármol y una terraza con vista panorámica a las montañas o al océano. Las sesiones de yoga meditativo en tiendas redondas, así como las conferencias sobre astrología y las terapias de spa en la habitación forman parte de la extraordinaria oferta.

Questo resort – vero consiglio da insider, tranquillo e tuttavia lussuosissimo – è situato a circa 365 metri sul livello del mare ed è gestito nel più completo rispetto dell'ambiente. Le case, arroccate sulla rupe in posizione appartata, risalgono la collina. Elementi moderni e rustici si fondono nel loro stile. Ogni casa è provvista di camino, vasca Jacuzzi di marmo e di una terrazza con vista panoramica sulle montagne e sull'oceano. L'esclusivo servizio comprende trattamenti Spa in camera, yoga meditativo in una iurta e conferenze di astrologia.

Half of the Inn's 30 rooms overlook the mountains; the rest offer a view of the Pacific Ocean.

Von der Hälfte der 30 Zimmer kann der Gast den Blick auf die Berge genießen, von der anderen Hälfte blickt er auf den Pazifischen Ozean.

De la moitié des 30 chambres, l'hôte profite de la vue sur les montagnes, de l'autre moitié, il contemple l'océan Pacifique.

Desde una parte de las 30 habitaciones el huésped podrá disfrutar de un paisaje de montañas y desde la otra asomarse al Océano Pacífico.

Da metà delle 30 camere si gode la vista sulle montagne, mentre l'altra metà si affaccia sull'oceano Pacifico.

The luxurious grass-roofed suites, tucked away into the landscape with stunning ocean views and majestic treescapes invite to relax.

Die luxuriösen Suiten laden zum Entspannen ein. Aufgrund ihres Grasdachs passen sie sich in die Landschaft ein, die mit fantastischen Meerblicken und majestätischen Bäumen aufwartet.

Les suites luxueuses invitent à la détente. Grâce à leur toit de verdure, elles se fondent dans le paysage, offrant une vue fantastique sur la mer et les arbres majestueux.

Las lujosas suites invitan a la relajación. Gracias a su techo de hierba se integran perfectamente en un paisaje que ofrece al huésped fabulosas vistas del mar y a árboles majestuosos.

Le lussuose suite invitano al relax. Con il loro tetto di erba, si integrano perfettamente in un paesaggio di alberi maestosi tra le cui fronde si intravede il mare.

Beverly Hills Hotel

Beverly Hills, California

Behind the famous façade, the Beverly Hills Hotel remains the star-studded haven it was in Hollywood's golden days. Known for its mythic garden bungalows and the legendary Polo Lounge, the hotel still remains one of the most secluded and luxurious residences by retaining its over-the-top glory. Its 204 rooms are all lavishly outfitted with state-of-the-art luxury, each uniquely decorated in a subdued palette of pinks, greens, apricots, and yellows, accented with its infamous banana leaf design.

Das Hotel ist untrennbar mit der goldenen Ära Hollywoods verbunden. Hinter seiner berühmten Fassade ist es noch heute ein sicherer Hafen für Stars. Bekannt für seine mythischen Garten-Bungalows und die legendäre Polo-Lounge, gehört es nach wie vor zu den privatesten und luxuriösesten Residenzen der Stadt. Die 204 Zimmer sind verschwenderisch mit modernem Luxus eingerichtet. Jeder Raum ist individuell in gedämpften Pink-, Grün-, Apricot- und Gelbtönen gestaltet, akzentuiert von dem populären Bananenblattdesign.

L'hôtel est indissociable de l'âge d'or d'Hollywood. Derrière sa célèbre façade, il constitue encore un havre protégé pour les stars. Connu pour ses bungalows mythiques entourés de jardins et le légendaire Polo Lounge, il fait toujours partie des résidences les plus privées et les plus luxueuses de la ville. Les 204 chambres sont dispendieusement aménagées dans un luxe moderne. Chaque pièce est individuelle, décorée dans des tons discrets, rose, vert, abricot et jaune, que vient souligner le célèbre design à la feuille de banane.

Este hotel está estrechamente unido a la época dorada de Hollywood. Tras su famosa fachada sigue siendo hoy día refugio para las estrellas. Conocido por sus míticos bungalows de jardín y el legendario Polo Lounge, este hotel conserva aún su reputación como una de las residencias más íntimas y lujosas de la ciudad. El mobiliario elegido para las 204 habitaciones es un derroche de lujo. Cada espacio está individualmente definido con discretos tonos rosa, verde, melocotón y amarillo, resaltando así, el reconocido diseño de hoja de banana.

Questo hotel è indissolubilmente legato all'era d'oro di Hollywood. La sua celebre facciata cela ancora oggi un ritiro sicuro per le star. Noto per i mitici bungalow, sparsi nel giardino, e la leggendaria Polo Lounge, è ancora oggi uno dei soggiorni più discreti e lussuosi della città. Le 204 camere sono riccamente arredate con oggetti prestigiosi e moderni. Ogni stanza è stata realizzata in stile individuale nei toni smorzati del rosa, del verde, dell'albicocca e del giallo, sottolineati dal famoso design con foglie di banano.

Ever since its opening in 1912, the infamous pink stucco Spanish-style mansion known as the "Pink Palace" remains a magnet for the Hollywood movie colony.

Seit seiner Eröffnung 1912 ist das Anwesen im spanischen Stil mit seinem charakteristischen pinkfarbenen Stuck als „Pink Palace" bekannt. Über die Jahre ist es ein Magnet für Filmleute geblieben.

Depuis l'ouverture en 1912, le domaine, de style espagnol, est surnommé le « Pink Palace » pour ses stucs roses. Au fil des ans il est resté un aimant pour le monde du cinéma.

Desde su inauguración en 1912, este edificio de estilo español es conocido como "el palacio rosa" por su famoso estuco en este color. Durante todo el año el hotel atrae a personajes del mundo del arte cinematográfico.

Sin dalla sua inaugurazione nel 1912, il resort, in stile spagnoleggiante, è noto come "Pink Palace" a causa del singolare edificio rosa che attirava e attira tuttora le stelle del cinema.

Legendary stars such as Marilyn Monroe, Howard Hughes, and Greta Garbo lived in the fabled private bungalows that are nestled within 12 acres of lush, tropical-like grounds.

Legendäre Persönlichkeiten wie Marilyn Monroe, Howard Hughes und Greta Garbo lebten in den sagenumwobenen privaten Bungalows, die auf dem rund fünf Hektar großen, tropisch bewachsenem Gelände verstreut liegen.

Des personnalités légendaires telles que Marilyn Monroe, Howard Hughes et Greta Garbo séjournèrent dans ces bungalows privés, nimbés de légendes et dispersés sur un terrain de presque cinq hectares de végétation tropicale.

Verdaderos mitos del cine como Marilyn Monroe, Howard Hughes y Greta Garbo vivieron en estos privados bungalows de leyenda, que se encuentran diseminados en un área de aproximadamente cinco hectáreas, rodeados de una exuberante vegetación tropical.

Autentici miti come Marilyn Monroe, Howard Hughes e Greta Garbo hanno vissuto nei leggendari e discreti bungalow sparsi nel giardino tropicale di circa cinque ettari.

Raffles L'Ermitage Beverly Hills

Beverly Hills, California

Contemporary luxury hotel with an Asian-meets-Scandinavian-style that exudes elegance. This hotel is one of Los Angeles' understated jewels amidst a quiet Beverly Hills residential neighborhood, making an Euro-Asian design statement with an air of New York cool. The 119 enormous rooms have blonde hardwood floors, modern, tightly upholstered furniture with rich fabrics, English sycamore paneling, and French doors that open to city or mountain views.

In diesem zeitgenössischen Luxus-Hotel trifft Asien auf Skandinavien, ein Stil, der besondere Eleganz ausstrahlt. Das Haus setzt auf Understatement. Es liegt inmitten eines ruhigen Teils von Beverly Hills. Neben dem europäisch-asiatischen Design zeigt sich ein Hauch New Yorker Coolness. Die 119 großen Zimmer haben helle Hartholzböden und englische Bergahornvertäfelungen. Die modernen Polstermöbel sind mit edlen Stoffen bezogen. Französische Türen geben den Blick auf die Stadt oder auf die Berge frei.

Dans cet hôtel de luxe contemporain, Asie et Scandinavie se rencontrent, créant un style d'une élégance particulière. L'établissement, situé au cœur d'un quartier tranquille de Beverly Hills, mise sur la discrétion. À côté du design asiatico-européen, on perçoit une touche de nonchalance new-yorkaise. Dans les 119 grandes chambres, le sol est en bois dur clair et les lambris anglais en érable. Les meubles rembourrés modernes sont garnis de superbes étoffes. Les portes à la française dégagent la vue sur la ville ou sur les montagnes.

En este hotel de lujo contemporáneo se mezclan los estilos asiático y escandinavo dando lugar a un singular ambiente de exquisita elegancia. La casa destaca por su sobriedad. El edificio se encuentra ubicado en una apacible zona de Beverly Hills. Junto al diseño euroasiático se percibe también la frescura del espíritu neoyorquino. Las 119 habitaciones tienen suelos claros de madera dura y revestimiento en madera de arce blanco inglés. Sus modernos muebles están tapizados con elegantes telas. Las puertas francesas brindan una panorámica urbana o al paisaje de montaña.

In questo hotel di lusso di stile contemporaneo l'Asia incontra la Scandinavia in un connubio di squisita eleganza. L'edificio, al centro di un tranquillo quartiere di Beverly Hills, è all'insegna dell'understatement. Il design euro-asiatico è impreziosito da un tocco di nonchalance newyorkese. Le 119 spaziose camere hanno pavimenti chiari di legno duro e pannellature di acero di montagna in stile inglese. I mobili imbottiti, di gusto moderno, sono rivestiti con stoffe pregiate. Porte francesi si aprono sul panorama della città o delle montagne.

Grey and beige lounges are cozy and inviting, displaying subtle Chinese art. A wall of original scripts of some well-known films hang above the crackling fireplace.

Die in Grau und Beige gehaltenen Lounges wirken gemütlich und einladend. Neben chinesischer Kunst gibt es über dem Kamin eine Wand mit originalen Manuskriptseiten von bekannten Filmen.

Tout de gris et beige, les salons respirent le confort et la détente. Outre de l'art chinois, il y a, au-dessus de la cheminée, un mur avec des pages originales de manuscrits de films célèbres.

Los tonos gris y beige de los lounges hacen de ellos estancias acogedoras y atrayentes. Además del arte chino, sobre la chimenea se puede admirar una pared con manuscritos originales de películas famosas.

Le lounge, in cui dominano le sfumature del grigio e del beige, sono calde e accoglienti, arredate con oggetti d'arte cinesi. La parete sul camino raccoglie pagine di copioni originali di celebri film.

The pool is a famed Bel Air see-and-be-seen scene; luxurious cabanas have wireless LAN, phone, and fax. The adjoining rooftop terrace is ideal for dining.

Der Pool gehört zu den beliebtesten Orten zum Sehen-und-gesehen-werden in Bel Air. Die luxuriösen Pool-häuschen sind mit wireless LAN, Telefon und Fax ausgestattet. Die angeschlossene Dachterrasse bietet sich zum Abendessen an.

La piscine est un des endroits favoris pour voir et être vu à Bel Air. Les pavillons luxueux de la piscine sont dotés de connexions LAN, de téléphone et de fax sans fil. La terrasse sur le toit adjacente est le lieu idéal pour le dîner.

La piscina es el escenario perfecto para observar y ser observado en Bel Air. Las lujosas casetas de la piscina están dotadas de red LAN inalámbrico, teléfono y fax. La terraza del ático invita a cenar.

La piscina è uno dei luoghi preferiti di Bel Air per vedere e farsi vedere. Le lussuose casette ai suoi bordi sono provviste di Wireless LAN, telefono e fax. La terrazza panoramica annessa è l'ambiente ideale per la cena.

The Ritz-Carlton, Laguna Niguel

Dana Point, California

Old World meets the Pacific Rim. This regal 4-story Mediterranean-style refuge is legendary for its luxury and magnificent setting in front of a 2-mile-long beach with ocean panoramas. Terraces are filled with colorful flower gardens throughout the well-tended property. A gorgeous marble fireplace stands in the silk-lined lobby, perfect for sipping a cocktail while watching the sunset.

Die Alte Welt trifft auf pazifisches Flair. Dieses majestätische, vier Stockwerke hohe Haus mit mediterraner Optik ist legendär für seinen Luxus und die fantastische Lage an einem drei Kilometer langen Strand mit herrlichem Ozean-Panorama. Das gepflegte Anwesen besticht durch die bunten Blumengärten. Im Zentrum der mit Seide ausgekleideten Lobby steht ein wunderschöner Marmorkamin. Die gemütliche Bar ist der perfekte Ort, um einen Cocktail zu trinken und gleichzeitig den Sonnenuntergang zu genießen.

Le vieux continent rencontre le charme du Pacifique. Cette majestueuse bâtisse de quatre étages à l'aspect méditerranéen est légendaire pour le luxe proposé et sa formidable position au bord d'une plage de trois kilomètres de long avec un merveilleux panorama sur l'océan. Le domaine, très soigné, enchante par ses jardins de fleurs multicolores. Au centre du foyer tapissé de soie se dresse une magnifique cheminée de marbre. Le bar convivial est l'endroit idéal pour savourer un cocktail en contemplant le coucher du soleil.

El viejo mundo se fusiona con el encanto del Pacífico. Esta majestuosa casa de cuatro plantas y aspecto mediterráneo es legendaria por su lujo y su fantástica ubicación en una playa de tres kilómetros con espléndidas vistas al océano. La cuidada propiedad seduce con sus jardines de flores multicolores. Justo en el centro del lobby revestido de seda se encuentra una maravillosa chimenea de mármol. El acogedor bar es perfecto para tomar un cóctel mientras se disfruta de la puesta del sol.

Il vecchio mondo incontra il fascino del Pacifico: questa maestosa casa di quattro piani in stile mediterraneo è famosa per il suo lusso e per la sua splendida posizione: si trova infatti su una spiaggia di tre chilometri con una magnifica vista dell'oceano. Il resort, perfettamente curato, incanta con i suoi giardini dai coloratissimi fiori. Al centro della lobby, dalle pareti rivestite di seta, si trova un magnifico camino di marmo. L'accogliente bar è il luogo ideale per ammirare il tramonto sorseggiando un cocktail.

Elegant European ambience and unobstructed views of the Pacific; the new ocean-view restaurant "162'" is named for its height above the low tide.

Das neue Restaurant bietet elegantes, europäisches Ambiente und eine unverbaute Aussicht auf den Pazifik. Der Name „162'" ist gleichzeitig die Höhe des Restaurants über dem Meeresspiegel.

Le nouveau restaurant offre, dans une atmosphère élégante et européenne, une vue dégagée sur le Pacifique. Le nom de « 162' » correspond à sa hauteur au-dessus du niveau de la mer.

El nuevo restaurante ofrece un elegante ambiente europeo, así como una directa vista al Pacífico. Su nombre, "162'", corresponde a su altura sobre el nivel del mar.

Un elegante ambiente di gusto europeo accoglie il nuovo ristorante, che ha libera vista sul Pacifico. Il nome "162'" corrisponde ai metri sul livello del mare.

393 rooms have interiors in sand tones, supplemented by cool palettes of blue and silver with magenta accents, and triple-layered glass panels that suggest an undersea world.

Die Einrichtung der 393 Zimmer ist in Sandtönen gehalten. Sie wird durch eine Palette kühler Blau- und Silbernuancen mit Akzenten in Magenta ergänzt. Dreischichtige Glaspaneele suggerieren eine Unterwasserwelt.

La décoration des 393 chambres privilégie les tons sablés. Elle se complète d'une palette de froides nuances bleu et argent avec des touches de magenta. Des panneaux à triple vitrage suggèrent un monde sous-marin.

Las 393 habitaciones están decoradas en color arena, combinado con una gama de matices de azul fresco y plata con reflejos magenta. Los paneles de cristal de triple capa sugieren un mundo submarino.

Nell'arredamento delle 393 camere prevale il colore sabbia, ravvivato dalle note fredde del blu e dell'argento e da tocchi di magenta. Pannelli di vetro a triplo strato evocano l'atmosfera del fondo del mare.

The Ritz-Carlton, Laguna Niguel *Dana Point, California* 55

The Parker Palm Springs

Palm Springs, California

Exotic and eclectic mid-century estate with landscaped gardens reminiscent of Versailles, updated for a design-savvy group who likes to congregate on the hammocks and around the four swimming pools. Behind its bold orange doors, the Zebra print rugs suits of armor, bear-skin lined chairs, and white-washed cinderblock walls complete its post modern look. All 144 rooms and villas showcase a retro-groovy design.

Das exotische und eklektische Anwesen, Mitte des 20. Jahrhunderts erbaut, wurde für designbewusste Gäste auf den neuesten Stand gebracht. In den landschaftlichen Gärten, die teilweise an Versailles erinnern, finden sich zahlreiche Hängematten und vier Pools. Hinter gewagten, orangefarbenen Türen liegen Teppiche mit Zebra-Print. Ritterrüstungen, mit Bärenfell bezogene Stühle und weiß getünchte Wände komplettieren den postmodernen Look. „Retro und Groovy" lautet das Motto auch in den 144 Zimmern und Villen.

Ce domaine exotique et éclectique, construit au milieu du 20ème siècle, a été modernisé pour des hôtes férus de design. Dans les jardins bucoliques qui rappellent parfois Versailles, on trouve de nombreux hamacs et quatre piscines. Derrière des portes hardiment peintes en orange se déroulent des tapis aux motifs zébrés. Des armures de chevalier, des chaises garnies de peaux d'ours et des murs badigeonnés de blanc complètent ce look postmoderne. « Groovy », c'est le thème qui prévaut aussi dans les 144 chambres et villas.

La exótica y ecléctica propiedad construida a mitad del s. XX fue reformada para huéspedes amantes del diseño. Los paisajísticos jardines, que en parte recuerdan a Versalles, albergan cuatro piscinas y numerosas hamacas. Tras las atrevidas puertas de color naranja descansan alfombras con estampados tipo cebra. Este "look" postmoderno lo complementan armaduras, sillas tapizadas en piel de oso y encaladas paredes blancas. Los temas retro y "groovy" también están presentes en las 144 habitaciones y villas.

Questa tenuta dallo stile esotico ed eclettico, costruita verso la metà del XX secolo, è stata completamente rimodernata per gli amanti del design. Numerose amache sono sparse qua e là nei pittoreschi giardini, realizzati nello stile di Versailles, che accolgono anche quattro piscine. Porte di un aggressivo color arancione si schiudono su un arredamento di gusto post-moderno, con tappeti zebrati, armature, sedie ricoperte di pelli d'orso e pareti imbiancate. Tipicamente "groovy" è anche l'atmosfera che pervade le 144 camere e ville.

A sculptural porte cochere, a white wall of concrete latticework constructed in Greco-Roman motif, is a welcoming first impression to Palm Spring's swankiest resort.

Ein skulpturgleicher Eingangsbereich: Eine weiße Gitterkonstruktion aus Beton mit griechisch-römischem Motiv ist die moderne Version eines Portikus und das Erste, was die Gäste vom mondänsten Resort in Palm Springs sehen.

Un hall d'entrée sculptural : une construction ajourée blanche en béton aux motifs gréco-romains constitue la version moderne du portique ; c'est ce que voient en premier les hôtes du plus mondain des resorts de Palm Springs.

Un portal escultural: Lo primero que salta a la vista en este elegante resort de Palm Springs es una reja blanca de hormigón con motivos greco-romanos, una versión moderna de lo que fuera un pórtico.

Un ingresso come una scultura: una cancellata di cemento bianco con motivi greco-romani, moderna versione di un portico, è la prima cosa che appare agli ospiti del resort più mondano di Palm Springs.

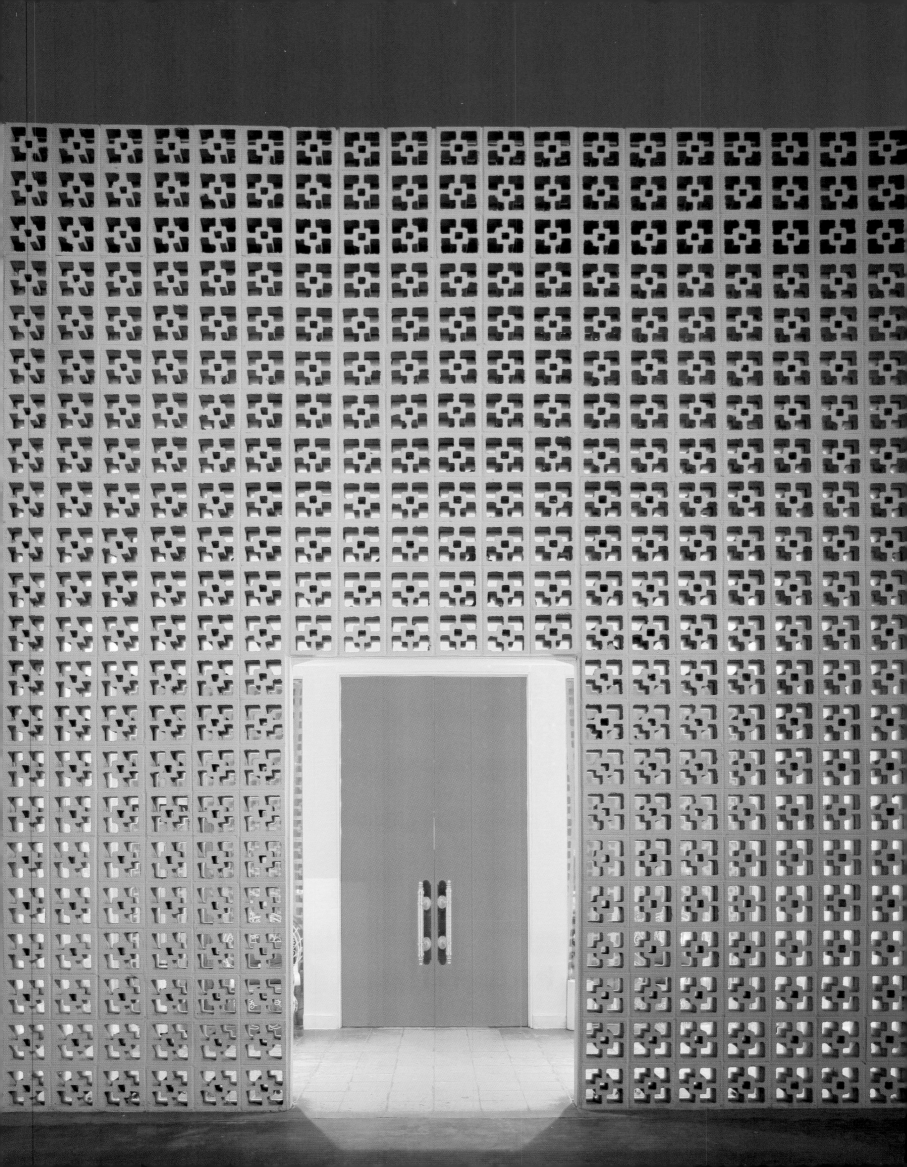

With no reception desk, a valet clerk escorts guests to their rooms, followed by a tour of the 13-acre grounds, including a communal fire pit which is surrounded by butterfly chairs.

Eine typische Rezeption fehlt. Ein Page begleitet die Gäste zu ihren Zimmern und zeigt ihnen das fünf Hektar große Gelände mit gemeinschaftlicher Feuerstelle, die von Stühlen mit Schmetterlingsmuster umgeben ist.

Il manque une réception traditionnelle. C'est un groom qui accompagne les hôtes à leur chambre et leur fait visiter le parc de cinq hectares et l'endroit aménagé pour les feux de bois, entouré de chaises en forme de papillon.

No existe la clásica recepción. Un botones acompaña a los huéspedes a sus habitaciones y les enseña el recinto de cinco hectáreas que cuenta con un fogaril común al aire libre rodeado de sillas con diseños de mariposa.

Non esiste una tipica reception. Un valletto accompagna gli ospiti alle proprie camere e mostra la tenuta di cinque ettari provvista di un braciere comune circondato da sedie con motivi a farfalle.

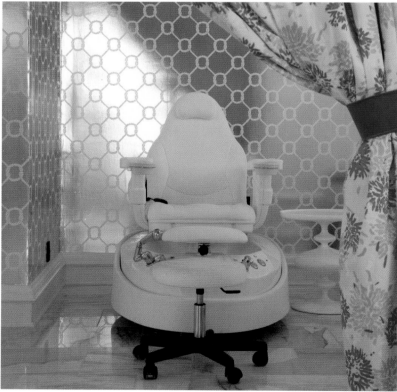

Each room has textured sisal floor coverings, exotic woven fabrics in bright colors, leather seating, vintage Hollywood photos, eclectic furnishings and designer toiletries.

In jedem Zimmer finden sich Sisalteppiche, exotische, gewebte Stoffe in leuchtenden Farben, alte Hollywood-Fotos, eklektisches Mobiliar und eine Designer-Badezimmerausstattung.

Dans chaque chambre il y a des tapis de sisal, des étoffes exotiques tissées aux couleurs vives, de vieilles photos de Hollywood, des meubles éclectiques et une salle de bain conçue par un designer.

Cada habitación está dotada de alfombras de sisal, tejidos exóticos de vivos colores, fotos antiguas de Hollywood, mobiliario ecléctico, así como un cuarto de baño de diseño.

In ogni camera si trovano tappeti di sisal, stoffe esotiche dai colori brillanti tessute a mano, vecchie foto di Hollywood, mobili eclettici e un bagno firmato da noti designer.

THEhotel
at Mandalay Bay

Las Vegas, Nevada

Rising from the southern tip of the Las Vegas strip next to Mandalay Bay, THEhotel is the city's first boutique, all-suite hotel that is completely casino free. The overall design emits a serene feel with its gray-and-black cosmopolitan interiors. Ultramodern 725-square-foot guest rooms all have floor-to-ceiling windows, three flat screen TVs, and exquisite marble and granite bathrooms. A cutting-edge restaurant called "Mix" is located on the top floor, offering an incredible view of the city.

An der südlichen Spitze des Las Vegas Strip, direkt neben der Mandalay Bay, erhebt sich das erste Suiten- und Boutique-Hotel der Stadt ohne Casino. Das Design strahlt, mit seiner in Grau und Schwarz gehaltenen, kosmopolitischen Einrichtung, eine gelassene Stimmung aus. Die ultramodernen, rund 68 Quadratmeter großen Zimmer haben Fenster vom Boden bis zur Decke, drei Flachbildfernseher sowie Badezimmer aus Marmor und Granit. Vom innovativen Restaurant „Mix" hat der Gast eine atemberaubende Aussicht über die Stadt.

A la pointe sud du strip de Las Vegas, directement à côté de Mandalay Bay, s'élève le premier hôtel-boutique avec suites de la ville, sans casino. Le design, avec sa décoration cosmopolite en noir et gris, crée une ambiance décontractée. Les chambres ultramodernes, d'environ 68 mètres carrés, sont dotées de portes-fenêtres du sol au plafond, de trois téléviseurs à écran plat et d'une salle de bain en marbre et en granit. Le restaurant « Mix », très innovant, garantit aux hôtes une vue à couper le souffle sur la ville.

En el extremo sur de Las Vegas Strip junto a Mandalay Bay, se alza el primer hotel boutique con suites de la ciudad que no tiene casino. El diseño, gracias al mobiliario cosmopolita negro-gris, contribuye a crear una atmósfera apacible. Las habitaciones ultramodernas de aproximadamente 68 metros cuadrados están dotadas de ventanas del suelo al techo, tres televisores de pantalla plana y un cuarto de baño de mármol y granito. El restaurante "Mix" ofrece al huésped una impresionante vista de la ciudad.

All'estremità meridionale della Las Vegas Strip, proprio accanto alla Mandalay Bay, è situato il primo boutique hotel con suite della città senza sala da gioco. Il design cosmopolita in nero e grigio suscita tranquillità. Le modernissime camere, di circa 68 metri quadrati, hanno finestre extradimensionate alte fino al soffitto, tre televisori a schermo piatto e bagni di marmo e granito. Dal ristorante "Mix", di gusto innovativo, si gode una vista mozzafiato sulla città.

The hotel offers a casino-free, black-marble-and-chrome lobby that is as calm and inviting as some kind of futuristic Art Déco chapel.

Die Lobby des Hotels ist in schwarzem Marmor und Chrome gehalten. Aufgrund des fehlenden Casinos wirkt sie ruhig und einladend, wie eine futuristische Art-déco-Kapelle.

Le hall d'entrée de l'hôtel est en marbre noir et en chrome. Comme il n'y a pas de casino, il donne une impression de calme et de sérénité, tel une chapelle Art déco futuriste.

El lobby del hotel está decorado en mármol negro y cromo. El hecho de no tener casino lo convierte en un lugar apacible y acogedor como si se tratara de una capilla futurista art déco.

La lobby dell'hotel, in marmo nero e cromo, ricorda una cappella futuristica in stile art déco: senza sala da gioco irradia un'atmosfera tranquilla e invitante.

The interiors of all 117 suites are decorated in a welcoming palette of rich browns and muted blue-greys.

Die Einrichtung aller 117 Suiten erscheint durch die Palette intensiver Braun- und gedeckter Blau-Grautöne äußerst elegant.

L'aménagement de l'ensemble des 117 suites est exceptionnellement élégant grâce à une palette de tons marron profond et de bleu adouci.

La decoración de las 117 suites es de extrema elegancia, gracias a una gama de tonos marrón intenso y un sobrio verde azulado.

Marrone intenso e sobri tocchi blu e grigi conferiscono all'arredamento delle 117 suite un carattere estremamente raffinato.

Sanctuary on Camelback Mountain

Scottsdale, Arizona

A boutique hideaway with dramatic mountain view and spa casitas terraced over 53 heavenly acres of exotic desert landscaping in the northern foothills of Camelback Mountain. Its cutting-edge design is a contemporary alternative to the more traditional Southwestern offerings in the area. Each of the 98 spa casitas are reminiscent of Indian pueblos, with squared, low lines and cast concrete walls.

Dieses Boutique-Refugium bietet eine dramatische Aussicht auf die Berge. Die kleinen Spa-Häuser liegen über 21 himmlischen Hektar exotischer Wüstenlandschaft in den nördlichen Ausläufern der Camelback Mountains verteilt. Mit seinem innovativen Design ist das Anwesen eine zeitgemäße Alternative zu den eher traditionell-südwestlichen Angeboten der Gegend. Jedes der 98 Häuschen erinnert an indianische Pueblos mit quadratischer Linienführung und gegossenen Betonwänden.

Ce sanctuaire-boutique offre une vue spectaculaire sur les montagnes. Les petits pavillons spa sont dispersés sur 21 merveilleux hectares d'un paysage exotique de désert sur les contreforts nord de Camelback Mountain. Son design novateur fait de ce domaine une alternative moderne aux établissements traditionnels du sud-ouest de la région. Chacune des 98 maisonnettes rappelle les villages indiens avec des formes carrées et des murs en béton coulé.

Este refugio boutique ofrece una impactante vista de las montañas. Las pequeñas casas spa se reparten por un maravilloso y exótico paisaje desértico de 21 hectáreas, situado en la vertiente norte de las montañas Camelback. Con su diseño innovador, el edificio constituye una alternativa moderna frente a la oferta de los alrededores, en una línea tradicional típica del sudoeste. Sus 98 casas recuerdan a pueblos indios de estructura cuadrada y moldeadas paredes de hormigón.

Da questo boutique hotel si gode una vista spettacolare sulle montagne. Le casette della Spa sono situate ai margini settentrionali delle Camelback Mountains, in uno straordinario paesaggio brullo ed esotico di 21 ettari. Il design innovativo di questo hotel è una valida alternativa a quello della parte sud-occidentale della regione, di tipo più tradizionale. Ognuna delle 98 villette, dalle linee squadrate e dalle pareti di cemento, è costruita a somiglianza di un pueblo indiano.

Contemporary design integrated with an Asian touch, infusing smooth lines of gold, stainless steel and accents of stone; the casitas are painted in desert hues of terracotta and bluegreen.

Das zeitgenössische Design hat einen asiatischen Touch — goldene Linien, rostfreier Stahl und Akzente aus Stein. Die Häuschen sind in Wüstentönen von Terrakotta bis Blaugrün schattiert.

Le design contemporain possède un charme asiatique — des lignes dorées, de l'acier inoxydable et des éléments de pierre. Les pavillons sont aux couleurs du désert, dans des tons allant de la terre cuite au bleu-vert.

El diseño actual tiene un toque asiático de trazos dorados, acero inoxidable y piedra. Las casas ofrecen tonalidades propias del desierto, desde terracota hasta verde azulado.

Il design, di gusto moderno, è arricchito da accenti asiatici: linee dorate, acciaio inossidabile e inserti in pietra. I colori ricoprono tutte le sfumature del deserto, dalla terracotta al verdeazzurro.

Walls of windows wrap around the restaurant and lounge and offers each seat in the house awe-inspiring views of Paradise Valley.

Fensterwände umgeben das Restaurant und die Lounge. So bietet jeder Platz im Raum einen erfurchtgebietenden Blick auf das Paradise Valley.

Des baies vitrées entourent le restaurant et le salon. Ainsi chaque emplacement garantit une vue imposante sur la Paradise Valley.

El restaurante y el lounge están rodeados de ventanales, que permiten disfrutar desde cualquier sitio de una fabulosa vista del Paradise Valley.

Il ristorante e la lounge sono circondati da vetrate: da ogni tavolo, si gode una magnifica vista su Paradise Valley.

*A **walkway*** of smooth black river rock and volcanic glass winds past brilliant desert flowers and prickly cactus and manicured gardens, passing a pool flowing off to infinity.

Ein Fußweg *aus glattem, schwarzen Fluss- und Vulkangestein windet sich entlang brillanter Wüstenblumen, stacheliger Kakteen und manikürter Gärten, vorbei an einem Pool, der in die Unendlichkeit zu fließen scheint.*

Un chemin, *pavé de pierre volcanique et de graviers noirs et lisses, serpente entre des fleurs du désert luisantes, des cactus épineux et des jardins bien entretenus, devant une piscine qui semble s'écouler vers l'infini.*

Un sendero *de planas y negras piedras volcánicas y cantos de río se desliza entre llamativas flores del desierto, espinosos cactus y cuidados jardines, pasando por una piscina que parece extenderse en la inmensidad.*

Un sentiero *di ghiaia nera e liscia, che si snoda tra fiori dai colori brillanti, cactus spinosi e giardini splendidamente curati, conduce anche ad una piscina che sembra perdersi nell'infinito.*

Hyatt Regency Scottsdale Resort and Spa at Gainey Ranch

Scottsdale, Arizona

A desert oasis shaded by towering palm trees with manicured gardens and paths. Here you will find water everywhere; an extravagant water playground serves as the resort's focal point. 10 interconnecting swimming pools are interlinked with waterways and an artificial sand beach. Stone, brick and coppery tones echo the natural Arizona landscape. The 2-story lobby, is open to a height of 17 feet and connected to outdoor conversation areas with stone fireplaces.

Eine Wüstenoase, beschattet von emporragenden Palmen mit exakt angelegten Gärten und Wegen. Das zentrale Element des Resorts ist Wasser: Die zehn Pools sind durch Wasserwege und künstliche Strände miteinander verbunden. Stein, Ziegel und Kupfertöne spiegeln die Landschaft Arizonas wider. Von der zweigeschossigen, fünf Meter hohen offenen Lobby blickt man auf gemütliche Feuerstellen aus Stein, die unter dem freien Himmel Raum zum Entspannen bieten.

Une oasis dans le désert, à l'ombre de hauts palmiers, avec jardins et allées soigneusement entretenus. L'élément central du resort est l'eau : les dix bassins sont reliés entre eux par des canaux et une plage artificielle. Les nuances roche, ardoise et cuivre reflètent le paysage de l'Arizona. Le hall de deux étages, presque cinq mètres de haut, est ouvert. De là, on aperçoit d'agréables endroits aménagés avec de la pierre pour des feux de bois qui permettent de se détendre en plein air.

Un oasis en el desierto protegido por altas palmeras, con estilizados jardines y senderos. El elemento central del resort es el agua: Las diez piscinas están conectadas a través de canales y playas artificiales. Las piedras, tejas y los tonos cobrizos reproducen el paisaje de Arizona. El lobby de dos plantas es abierto y tiene una altura de 5 metros. Desde aquí se divisan unos acogedores fogariles de piedra que, al aire libre, invita a la relajación.

All'ombra di palme lussureggianti, tra giardini e sentieri meravigliosamente curati, si trova questa oasi nel deserto. L'elemento di questo resort è l'acqua: le dieci piscine sono collegate le une alle altre da torrentelli e spiagge artificiali. Nei colori della pietra, del mattone e del rame si rispecchia il paesaggio dell'Arizona. La lobby, a due piani, è aperta fino ad un'altezza di cinque metri. Accoglienti bracieri di pietra invitano alla sosta e al relax sotto il cielo.

This desert resort is set amidst hundreds of palm trees and flowering cactus surrounding the pools, all framed against the majestic McDowell Mountains.

Das Wüsten-Resort wurde inmitten Hunderter Palmen errichtet und blühende Kakteen umgeben die Pools — den Hintergrund bilden die majestätischen McDowell Mountains.

Ce resort du désert a été construit au milieu de centaines de palmiers. Des cactus en fleurs entourent les bassins — en toile de fond se dressent les imposantes montagnes McDowell.

El resort del desierto surge entre cientos de palmeras y cactus en flor que rodean las piscinas, con las majestuosas McDowell Mountains como telón de fondo.

Il resort nel deserto è stato costruito tra centinaia di palme; cactus in fiore circondano le piscine da cui si gode la vista delle maestose McDowell Mountains.

Vibrant, yet calm color tones and fabrics promote drama and excitement. Greens, reds, and ambers—all inspired by the natural surroundings.

Ruhige und doch pulsierende Farben und Materialien unterstreichen die beeindruckende Kulisse. Die Grün-, Rot- und Ambertöne sind von der Umgebung inspiriert.

Paisibles mais aussi dynamiques, les couleurs et les matériaux soulignent la beauté du décor. Les tons vert, rouge et ambre sont inspirés par l'environnement.

Suaves pero palpitantes colores y materiales realzan el fascinante escenario. Los tonos verde, rojo y ámbar están inspirados en el entorno.

Materiali e colori naturali e accesi arricchiscono questo scenario spettacolare: le sfumature verdi, rosse e ambrate si ispirano al paesaggio.

The Ritz-Carlton, South Beach

Miami Beach, Florida

In 1953, the DiLido Hotel opened in a top beach location. The design secured Morris Lapidus, an exponent of the Miami Modern style (MiMo), a place in architectural history. During the 200 million dollar restoration by the Ritz-Carlton Hotel Company, particular care was taken to retain as many of the historic elements as possible: the concave interior and exterior walls, the pastel accents and the 'amoeba' shapes on the ceilings and walls. Luxury yacht design inspired the decor in the hotel's 376 rooms.

Mit dem DiLido Hotel, das 1953 in bester Strandlage eröffnet wurde, schrieb Morris Lapidus, Vertreter des Designstils Miami Modern (MiMo), Architekturgeschichte. Bei der aufwändigen 200 Millionen Dollar teuren Renovierung durch die Ritz-Carlton Hotel Company wurde darauf geachtet, möglichst viel von der historischen Bausubstanz zu erhalten: die konkaven Innen- und Außenwände, die typischen Pastellfarben, die amöbenförmigen Ausschnitte an Decken und Wänden. Das Interieur der 376 Zimmer ist der Gestaltung von Luxusyachten entlehnt.

Avec le DiLido Hotel, inauguré en 1953 et possédant un emplacement idéal sur la plage, Morris Lapidus, représentant du style design Miami Modern (MiMo) a écrit une page de l'histoire de l'architecture. Lors de la rénovation effectuée par la Ritz-Carlton Hotel Company qui a coûté 200 millions de dollars, les architectes ont veillé à conserver le plus possible la substance historique du bâtiment : les parois intérieures et extérieures concaves, les couleurs pastel typiques, les détails des plafonds et des murs en forme d'amibes. L'intérieur des 376 chambres s'inspire de l'aménagement des yachts de luxe.

Con el hotel DiLido, inaugurado en 1953 en el mejor lugar de la playa, el arquitecto Morris Lapidus, representante del estilo arquitectónico Miami Modern (MiMo), hizo historia. Durante la renovación a cargo de la compañía hotelera Ritz-Carlton Hotel Company, estimada en 200 millones de dólares, se dedicó especial atención a la conservación de la estructura histórica del edificio: Las paredes cóncavas interiores y exteriores, los típicos colores pastel, los fragmentos en forma de ameba del techo y las paredes. El interior de las 376 habitaciones se inspira en el diseño de los yates de lujo.

Quando il DiLido Hotel aprendo nel 1953 si guadagnò uno dei migliori posti al sole, il suo realizzatore Morris Lapidus, rappresentante della corrente di design conosciuta come Miami Modern (MiMo), inaugurava un nuovo capitolo nella storia dell'architettura. L'onerosa ristrutturazione operata dalla catena alberghiera Ritz-Carlton Hotel Company con costi pari a 200 milioni di dollari ha tenuto in massimo conto la struttura architettonica storica di cui ha cercato di preservare il più possibile: le pareti interne ed esterne concave, le tipiche tonalità pastello, i dettagli a forma di ameba ai soffitti e alle pareti. Gli interni delle 376 stanze si ispirano all'arredamento degli yacht di lusso.

Morris Lapidus's work is instantly recognizable. With its 72 domed sconces, the polished cherry wood wall in the hotel lobby enjoys particular acclaim.

Unverkennbar ist die Formensprache von Morris Lapidus, legendär die hochglanzpolierte Kirschholzwand in der Hotelhalle mit den 72 kuppelförmigen Wandleuchten.

Le langage des formes de Morris Lapidus est indéniable, le mur en cerisier poli brillant dans le hall de l'hôtel avec ses 72 lampes murales en forme de coupoles est légendaire.

Inconfundible es el lenguaje de las formas de Morris Lapidus, legendaria la reluciente pared de madera de cerezo en el vestíbulo del hotel con las 72 lámparas de techo en forma de cúpula.

Inconfondibile il linguaggio estetico-formale di Morris Lapidus, leggendaria la parete di ciliegio tirata a lucido nella hall dell'hotel con le sue 72 applique emisferiche.

Beach life at its most luxurious: alongside poolside beds that can be hired on a daily basis, a pair of tanning butlers are on hand for all your bronzing needs.

Strandleben von seiner luxuriösen Seite: „Daybeds", die man tageweise mieten kann, und zwei „Tanning-Butler", deren Equipment an Sonnencremes keinen Wunsch offen lässt.

La vie à la plage côté luxe : des lits que l'on peut louer à la journée, ainsi que deux « tanning-butlers » dont le choix de crèmes solaires satisfera tous les visiteurs.

Las propuestas más lujosas para la playa: Las "daybeds", que se pueden alquilar por días y dos "tanning butlers", cuyo surtido de cremas solares satisface todos los gustos.

Vita da spiaggia nella sua accezione più lussuosa: lettini da sole affittabili giornalmente e due "Tanning Butlers" dotati di un assortimento di creme solari in grado di esaudire ogni richiesta.

The Raleigh Hotel
Miami Beach, Florida

An elegant, discreet and luxurious hotel in a simple yet stunning streamline 1940s style, restored to its original Art Déco design by hotelier André Balazs, but radiating a cool, laid-back feeling that is rare in glitzy South Beach. This 104-room oceanfront hotel boasts the area's most beautiful and famous fleur-de-lis shaped pool. Polished wood, original terrazzo floors, and an intimate martini bar add to the fabulous atmosphere.

Das elegante, diskrete Haus wurde von Hotelier André Balazs im geradlinigen und doch sehr eindrucksvollen Stil der 40er Jahre renoviert. Mit seinem Art-déco-Design strahlt es eine entspannte, kühle Atmosphäre aus, die im glitzernden South Beach eher selten ist. Es liegt direkt am Ozean. In dem Hotel mit 104 Zimmern ist man besonders stolz auf den Pool in Fleur-de-Lis-Form, den schönsten der Gegend. Glänzendes Holz, original Terrazzo-Böden und eine intime Martini-Bar tragen zur außergewöhnlichen Stimmung bei.

Élégant et discret, cet établissement a été rénové par l'hôtelier André Balazs dans le style rectiligne et pourtant très impressionnant des années 1940. Avec son design Art déco, il dégage une atmosphère froide et décontractée, plutôt rare parmi les scintillements de South Beach. Situé directement au bord de l'océan, l'hôtel, qui comprend 104 chambres, est particulièrement fier de sa piscine en forme de fleur de lys, la plus belle de la région. Des bois brillants, des sols en terrazzo véritable et un bar Martini intime contribuent à créer une ambiance exceptionnelle.

Esta elegante y discreta residencia fue reformada por el hotelero André Balazs en consonancia con el impresionante estilo de los años 40. El estilo art déco crea una atmósfera fresca y relajante, poco frecuente en la destellante South Beach. Este hotel situado frente al océano, cuenta con 104 habitaciones. La piscina en forma de flor de lis, considerada la más bella de la región, es uno de los motivos de orgullo del lugar. La madera reluciente, el suelo de terrazo original y un Martini bar contribuyen a crear un ambiente de exclusividad.

Questo hotel elegante e discreto è stato ristrutturato dal proprietario André Balazs nello stile lineare e tuttavia imponente degli anni 1940. Il design art déco evoca un'atmosfera tranquilla e rilassata piuttosto rara nella scintillante South Beach. L'hotel, che dispone di 104 camere, è situato direttamente sull'oceano: una particolare attrazione è la piscina a forma di fiordaliso, la più bella della zona. Legno lucente, pavimenti terrazzo originali e un bar Martini dall'atmosfera accogliente conferiscono al resort un fascino particolare.

This lushly landscaped South Beach hotel is a true tropical paradise with an old Havana theme, with bold colors, rattan and cane furniture, and brown and ocher terrazzo floors.

Das Hotel in South Beach ist mit seinen üppigen Grünanlagen ein wahres tropisches Paradies. Mit seinen Farben, den Rattan- und Schilfrohrmöbeln sowie den braunen und ockerfarbenen Terrazzo-Böden erinnert es an Havanna.

Le South Beach Hotel est un authentique paradis tropical avec son parc à la végétation luxuriante. Ses couleurs, les meubles de rotin et de roseau ainsi que les sols en terrazzo brun et ocre rappellent La Havane.

Este hotel en South Beach, situado en una voluptuosa zona ajardinada, es un verdadero paraíso tropical. Los colores, los muebles de ratán y junco, así como los suelos de terrazo marrón y tonos ocre recuerdan a La Habana.

Con i suoi giardini lussureggianti, il South Beach Hotel è un vero paradiso tropicale; i colori, i mobili in rattan e in vimini e i pavimenti terrazzo marrone e ocra ricordano l'atmosfera di L'Avana.

Six feet of sand was added to the garden to give guests better views from the remarkable pool famous for Esther Williams' aquatic film scenes from the 1940's.

Fast zwei Meter hoch wurde Sand im Garten aufgeschüttet, um den Gästen einen besseren Blick vom außergewöhnlichen Pool zu geben. Dieser ist bekannt für Esther Williams Wasserfilmszenen aus den 40er Jahren.

Presque deux mètres de sable ont été déversés dans le jardin pour offrir aux hôtes une meilleure vue à partir de l'exceptionnelle piscine. Celle-ci est célèbre pour les scènes de film dans l'eau d'Esther Williams dans les années 1940.

En el jardín se construyó un terraplén de arena de casi dos metros con el fin de ofrecer a los huéspedes mejores vistas desde la espléndida piscina, famosa por las escenas acuáticas de las películas de Esther Williams en los años 40.

Un terrapieno di sabbia di circa due metri è stato innalzato nel giardino per permettere agli ospiti di godere di una vista migliore dalla splendida piscina, nota per le scene girate da Esther Williams negli anni 1940.

The Setai

Miami Beach, Florida

This meticulously replicated Art déco landmark from the 1930s is now the hippest hotel to hit Miami's glitziest neighborhood, set amid tropical gardens and sparkling pools. Glinting mother-of-pearl make up the mile-long bar counter, and door handles are covered with stingray skin. The 125 spacious suites have Oriental décor, with Thai silk headboards and Indonesian ebony furniture.

Mit Liebe zum Detail wurde dieses Art-déco-Schmuckstück aus den 30er Jahren hergerichtet. Es ist gehört zu den angesagtesten Hotels der Stadt und liegt inmitten eines tropischen Gartens mit sprudelnden Pools. Schimmerndes Perlmutt macht die meterlange Theke zum Hingucker. Die Türgriffe sind mit Stachelrochenhaut bezogen. Die 125 Suiten bestechen durch ihr orientalisches Dekor. Mit Thai-Seide bespannte Kopfteile der Betten gehören genauso dazu wie indonesische Ebenholzmöbel.

C'est avec l'amour du détail que ce bijou de l'Art déco datant des années 1930 a été réaménagé. Il est l'un des hôtels les plus recherchés de la ville et se trouve au milieu d'un jardin tropical avec des piscines bouillonnantes. La nacre brillante ornant le comptoir long de plusieurs mètres attire les regards. Les poignées de porte sont revêtues de peau de pastenague. Le décor oriental des 125 suites est éblouissant ; les têtes de lit sont tendues de soie thaïlandaise et les meubles indonésiens en ébène.

Esta joya del art déco de los años 30 ha sido decorada con todo lujo de detalles. Es uno de los hoteles de moda de la ciudad y está situado en medio de un jardín tropical con piscinas burbujeantes. El nácar reluciente convierte la extensa barra en un objeto digno de admiración. Las manillas de las puertas están recubiertas con piel de pastinacas. Las 125 suites seducen con su decoración oriental. Tanto los cabeceros de la cama revestidos de seda tailandesa como el mobiliario en madera de ébano de Indonesia se integran perfectamente en el ambiente.

Questo gioiello di art déco fu costruito negli anni 1930 con grande amore per il particolare. È uno degli hotel più in voga della città ed è situato al centro di un giardino tropicale con zampilli e giochi d'acqua. Il lunghissimo banco è in lucente madreperla, mentre le maniglie delle porte sono rivestite di pelle di razza spinosa. Le 125 stanze e suite incantano con le loro decorazioni di gusto orientale, come le testiere ricoperte di seta tailandese o i mobili di ebano indonesiano.

For the *quintessential Miami Beach experience, guests lounge beside any of the three pools and order drinks from the 90-foot bar.*

Die ultimative *Miami-Beach-Erfahrung: Entspannen an einem der drei Pools und einen Drink von der 27 Meter langen Bar ordern.*

Le nec *plus ultra à Miami Beach : se détendre au bord d'une des trois piscines et commander une boisson au bar qui fait 27 mètres de long.*

La última *sensación en Miami Beach: Relajarse alrededor de una de las tres piscinas o disfrutar de una copa en el bar de 27 metros.*

L'ultimo grido *di Miami-Beach: rilassarsi ai bordi di una delle tre piscine ed ordinare un drink al banco del bar, lungo 27 metri.*

The original low-rise Art déco building is accompanied by a soaring 40-story, blue-glass-clad tower, part hotel, part luxury condominiums.

Zum originalen, flachen Art-déco-Gebäude gehört ein 40 Stockwerke hoher Turm, der mit blauem Glas verkleidet ist. In ihm befinden sich sowohl Hotelzimmer als auch Luxus-Eigentumswohnungen.

Le bâtiment plat d'origine de style Art déco s'est vu adjoindre une tour de 40 étages, revêtue de verre bleu. Celle-ci abrite des chambres d'hôtel ainsi que des appartements de luxe en copropriété.

Una torre de 40 pisos cubierta con cristal azul también pertenece al edificio plano original art déco. En ella están ubicadas las habitaciones y los lujosos pisos privados.

L'edificio piatto di stile art déco ha una torre di 40 piani rivestita di vetro azzurro in cui si trovano sia camere dell'hotel sia lussuosi appartamenti di proprietà.

Park Hyatt Chicago
Chicago, Illinois

Situated above Water Tower Square this hotel has 198 suites and 13 rooms. When the icy winds from Lake Michigan whistle past the skyscrapers, the cushioned ledges by the windows provide cozy lookouts for watching the hustle and bustle below. Designed by Culpepper, McAuliffe and Meaders the decor radiates exclusivity with its earthy tones. It also provides the perfect backdrop for the hotel's art collection, put together with help from the Museum of Contemporary Art and the Art Institute of Chicago.

Selbst wenn rasierklingenscharfer, eisiger Wind vom Michigan-See um die Hochhäuser pfeift, sind die gepolsterten Fenstersimse der 198 Suiten und 13 Zimmer ein perfekter Platz, um das Treiben um den Water Tower Square zu beobachten. Die von Culpepper, McAuliffe and Meaders in Erd- und Sandtönen gehaltene Innenarchitektur strahlt Exklusivität aus und bietet den richtigen Rahmen für die Kunstsammlung, die man zusammen mit dem Museum of Contemporary Art und dem Art Institute of Chicago ausgewählt hat.

Même si le vent glacial à couper au couteau du lac Michigan siffle entre les immeubles, les rebords rembourrés des fenêtres des 198 suites et treize chambres sont l'endroit idéal pour observer l'agitation caractérisant le Water Tower Square. Les nuances sable et terre pour lesquels ont opté Culpepper, McAuliffe et Meaders pour l'architecture intérieure dégagent une certaine exclusivité et créent un cadre idéal pour la collection d'objets d'art qui ont été choisis en collaboration avec le Museum of Contemporary Art et le Art Institute of Chicago.

Aun cuando el viento helado del lago Michigan pasa silbando por los edificios, los tapizados poyetes de las ventanas en las 198 suites y 13 habitaciones son un lugar ideal para observar el movimiento entorno a la Water Tower Square. La arquitectura interior al estilo de Culpepper, McAuliffe y Meaders en tonos tierra y arena irradia distinción y ofrece el marco ideal para la colección de arte seleccionada conjuntamente con el Museum of Contemporary Art y el Art Institute of Chicago.

Perfino quando il vento tagliente e gelido proveniente dal Lago Michigan soffia radente ai grattacieli, il posto ideale da cui osservare il viavai che anima Water Tower Square è dalle comode sedute imbottite alle finestre delle nove suite e 193 stanze dell'hotel. L'architettura d'interni, firmata Culpepper, McAuliffe and Meaders e tutta all'insegna delle cromie modulate sui toni terra e sabbia, comunica un senso di esclusività e crea la cornice perfetta per la collezione di opere d'arte selezionate con il supporto del Museum of Contemporary Art e dell'Art Institute of Chicago.

The seventh floor is home to the hotel spa and the NoMI restaurant. With a fine selection of wines and interior design by Tony Chi, this gastronomic beacon is one of the most popular dining spots in the city.

In der siebten Etage befinden sich das Spa und das Restaurant NoMI. Mit seiner Weinauswahl und dem von Designer Tony Chi entworfenen Ambiente ist es einer der beliebtesten Dining-Spots der Stadt.

Le spa et le restaurant NoMI se trouvent au septième étage. Grâce à sa sélection des vins et à l'ambiance créée par le designer Tony Chi, il s'agit de l'un des lieux de restauration les plus appréciés de la ville.

En el séptimo piso se encuentra el spa y el restaurante NoMI. Su selección de vinos y el ambiente creado por el diseñador Tony Chi hacen de este restaurante uno de los rincones para cenar preferidos de la ciudad.

Al settimo piano si trovano la Spa ed il ristorante NoMI, che grazie alla sua carta dei vini e all'atmosfera creata dal designer Tony Chi è diventato uno dei locali più "in" della città.

Sliding doors *separate bathrooms from bedrooms; NoMI Restaurant overlooks Water Tower Square, while the lounge offers great views of Michigan Avenue.*

Bad- und *Schlafzimmer sind durch Schiebewände getrennt; vom NoMI-Restaurant überblickt man den Water Tower Square, von der Lounge die Michigan Avenue.*

Les salles *de bain et les chambres sont séparées par des parois coulissantes ; dans le restaurant NoMI, on peut admirer le Water Tower Square. Dans le lounge, la vue sur la Michigan Avenue est superbe.*

El cuarto *de baño y el dormitorio están separados por paredes corredizas. Desde el restaurante NoMI se divisa la Water Tower Square y desde el lounge la Michigan Avenue.*

Bagni e *stanze sono separati da pareti scorrevoli. Dal ristorante NoMI, si gode di vista sul Water Tower Square, dal lounge, si può ammirare la Michigan Avenue.*

The Peninsula Chicago

Chicago, Illinois

This luxury hotel owned by the Peninsula Group is located right beside Chicago's iconic Tribune Tower along the "Magnificent Mile". The design was inspired by the Art déco style so popular in the city during the 1920s and 1930s. Murano glass lights and hand-polished stone tiles conjure up an elegant ambience, while the culinary highlight is the orientally themed Shanghai Terrace—a contemporary interpretation of an exclusive dining club from 1930s Shanghai.

An der Magnificent Mile, in direkter Nachbarschaft zum Chicagoer Wahrzeichen, dem Tribune Tower, liegt das zur Peninsula-Gruppe gehörende Luxus-Hotel. Das Design orientiert sich am Stil des Art déco, der in den 20er und 30er Jahren das Stadtbild Chicagos prägte. Leuchten aus Murano-Glas und handpolierte Steinfliesen kreieren ein edles Ambiente. Highlight des Restaurants ist die asiatische Shanghai-Terrasse, die zeitgenössische Version eines exklusiven Dinnerclubs aus dem Shanghai der 30er Jahre.

C'est sur la Magnificent Mile, à proximité directe de l'emblème de Chicago, la Tribune Tower, que se trouve l'hôtel de luxe appartenant au groupe Peninsula. Le design s'inspire du style Art déco qui caractérisait l'image de la ville dans les années 1920 et les années 1930. Les lampes en verre Murano et le carrelage en pierre poli à la main créent une ambiance recherchée. L'attraction du restaurant est la terrasse asiatique Shanghai, version contemporaine d'un club-restaurant exclusif du Shanghai des années 1930.

En la Magnificent Mile, muy cerca del monumento característico de Chicago, la Tribune Tower, se encuentra este hotel de lujo, propiedad del grupo Peninsula. Su diseño es de tendencia art déco, característico del Chicago de los años 20 y 30. Las lámparas de murano y baldosas de piedra pulidas a mano crean un ambiente exclusivo. Lo más llamativo del restaurante es su asiática terraza Shanghai, una versión moderna de los "dinnerclubs" del Shanghai de los años 30.

Affacciato sul Magnificent Mile, nelle dirette vicinanze della Tribune Tower, simbolo della città di Chicago: questa l'ubicazione d'eccezione dell'hotel di lusso della catena Peninsula. Il design trae ispirazione dallo stile art déco che negli anni 1920 e 1930 ha dato un'impronta inconfondibile alla città di Chicago. Le lampade in vetro di Murano e le mattonelle di pietra levigate a mano danno all'ambiente un tocco ricercato. Un vero highlight è il ristorante asiatico Shanghai Terrace, un dinnerclub esclusivo stile Shanghai anni 1930 rivisitato in chiave contemporanea.

As well as a huge indoor pool, the two-story hotel spa boasts floor-to-ceiling windows that offer stunning views of North Michigan Avenue.

Die über zwei Stockwerke reichende Fensterfront des Spas mit seinem großzügigen Indoor-Pool gibt einen fantastischen Blick auf die North Michigan Avenue frei.

La façade de fenêtres haute de deux étages du spa, doté d'une piscine intérieure généreuse, offre une vue sensationnelle sur la North Michigan Avenue.

La fachada de vidrio del spa, que ocupa dos pisos, con su amplia piscina interior, ofrece una vista fantástica sobre la North Michigan Avenue.

La facciata vetrata alta oltre due piani della Spa, dotata di ampia piscina interna, permette di spaziare con lo sguardo sulla North Michigan Avenue.

All 339 rooms and suites have luxurious, generously sized marble bathtubs. A glass installation by the artist Paul Housberg sets a distinctive tone in the hotel lobby.

Sämtliche 339 Zimmer und Suiten verfügen über komfortable, großzügige Marmorbäder. Die Glasinstallation des Künstlers Paul Housberg setzt im Eingangsbereich des Hotels einen markanten Akzent.

Les 339 chambres et suites disposent de salles de bain en marbre confortables et généreuses. L'installation en verre de l'artiste Paul Housberg donne un accent particulier au hall d'entrée de l'hôtel.

Las 339 habitaciones y suites cuentan con amplios y confortables cuartos de baño en mármol. Las instalaciones de vidrio del artista Paul Housberg aportan un toque especial a la entrada del hotel.

Tutte le 339 stanze e suite dispongono di spaziosi e confortevoli bagni in marmo. Di grande impatto l'installazione in vetro dell'artista Paul Housberg all'ingresso.

Sofitel Chicago Watertower
Chicago, Illinois

Designed by Jean-Paul Viguier, this distinctive hotel is somewhat of a landmark in Chicago's Near North Side. The inviting curved base of its glass exterior virtually steers passers-by into the lobby and the hotel's "Café des Architectes" restaurant. The latticed window pattern outside is complemented by an array of textures and gemstone-colored materials inside. During the day, light floods in to the rooms through the two main sides of the hotel, which taper into a sharp south-east-facing point.

Mit seinem charakteristischen Profil ist das von Jean-Paul Viguier entworfene Hotel eine Art Wahrzeichen des Stadtviertels Near North. Der ausladend geschwungene untere Teil der Glasfassade schiebt Passanten quasi in die Lobby und in das mit ihr verknüpfte Restaurant „Café des Architectes" hinein. Im Innern stehen dem rechtwinkeligen Gitter der Fassade eine Vielzahl von Texturen und edelsteinfarbenen Stoffen gegenüber. Viel Tageslicht durchflutet die Räume durch die beiden nach Südosten hin spitz zusammenlaufenden Fassaden.

Avec son profil caractéristique, l'hôtel conçu par Jean-Paul Viguier est une sorte d'emblème du quartier Near North. La partie inférieure arquée et en saillie de la façade en verre attire quasiment les passants pour les faire entrer dans le lobby et dans le restaurante « Café des Architectes » qui y est relié. À l'intérieur, un grand nombre de textures et de tissus couleur ivoire sont opposés à la grille rectangulaire de la façade. Une quantité importante de lumière naturelle inonde les pièces par les deux façades qui se réunissent en direction du sud-est pour former une pointe.

El perfil característico de este hotel diseñado por Jean-Paul Viguier le convierte en emblema del sector Near North. La prominente y arqueada parte baja de la fachada de vidrio casi empuja a los transeúntes hacia el lobby que conecta con el restaurante "Café des Architectes". El interior, frente a la reja rectangular de la fachada, se encierra una variedad de texturas y telas en colores de piedras preciosas. La luz del sol inunda las habitaciones a través de las fachadas, cuyos extremos convergen en dirección sudeste.

Grazie al suo peculiare profilo esterno, l'hotel progettato da Jean-Paul Viguier è diventato una sorta di simbolo del quartiere Near North. La parte inferiore aggettante della facciata in vetro si protende sopra il marciapiede, regalando la strana sensazione che i passanti stiano passeggiando nella lobby o nel ristorante "Cafè des Architectes" ad essa collegato. All'interno fanno da pendant al reticolo quadrangolare della facciata tutta una serie di accorgimenti e di tessuti nelle tonalità delle pietre preziose. La luce del giorno filtra abbondante attraverso le due facciate che convergono verso sud-est fino a toccarsi.

415 rooms and suites are spread across 32 floors. Most offer stunning panoramic views of the city.

415 Zimmer und Suiten sind auf 32 Stockwerke verteilt, die meisten von Ihnen bieten eine Panorama-Aussicht über die Stadt.

415 chambres et suites sont réparties sur 32 étages, la plupart d'entre elles offrent une vue panoramique sur la ville.

Las 415 habitaciones y suites están distribuidas en 32 pisos; la mayoría de ellas ofrece una vista panorámica de la ciudad.

Le 415 stanze e suite sono suddivise su 32 piani ed offrono in maggior parte vista panoramica sulla città.

When designing the hotel suites, interior architect Pierre-Yves Rochon drew inspiration from classic modern styles.

Bei der Gestaltung der Suiten setzte Innenarchitekt Pierre-Yves Rochon auf die klassische Moderne.

Pour l'aménagement des suites, l'architecte intérieur Pierre-Yves Rochon a opté pour un style moderne classique.

Para el diseño de las suites el arquitecto de interiores Pierre-Yves Rochon se ha inspirado en el modernismo clásico.

Per l'arredamento delle suite, l'architetto di interni Pierre-Yves Rochon ha puntato su un'interpretazione classico-moderna.

Fifteen Beacon

Boston, Massachusetts

Situated in the heart of Boston, this beaux arts building from 1903 presents a peerless mix of personal service par excellence and an intimacy usually associated with a private residence. 60 studios and suites, furnished with every conceivable comfort, are spread across a total of ten floors. The wine cellar is also home to the hotel restaurant. House specialties are pepped up with herbs grown in the hotel's very own roof garden, and served with a gem from the exquisite wine list.

In Bostons Zentrum verbirgt sich hinter der Beaux-Arts-Fassade aus dem Jahre 1903 eine perfekte Mischung aus unvergleichlichem Service und der Zurückgezogenheit einer privaten Residenz. Auf insgesamt zehn Stockwerken verteilen sich 60 Studios und Suiten, die mit allem erdenklichen Komfort ausgestattet sind. Der Weinkeller beherbergt zugleich das Restaurant des Hotels. Hier werden Spezialitäten des Hauses mit Kräutern aus dem eigenen Garten, der sich auf dem Dach des Gebäudes befindet, verfeinert und zu Spitzenweinen serviert.

Dans le centre de Boston, la façade Beaux-Arts de 1903 dissimule l'association parfaite du service incomparable et de la retraite d'une résidence privée. 60 studios et suites, équipés de tout le confort imaginable, sont répartis sur les dix étages du bâtiment. La cave à vin héberge également le restaurant de l'hôtel. Les spécialités de la maison sont servies avec des vins de grande qualité et assaisonnées avec les herbes du jardin de l'hôtel qui se trouve sur le toit du bâtiment.

En el centro de Boston, escondida tras la fachada Beaux Arts del año 1903, se da la combinación perfecta de un servicio único y la intimidad de una residencia privada. A través de diez pisos se extienden los 60 estudios y suites, equipados con todo el confort imaginable. La bodega alberga al mismo tiempo el restaurante del hotel. Aquí se sirven las especialidades de la casa aderezadas con finas hierbas, cosecha del propio jardín situado en la azotea del edificio, y acompañadas con vinos de élite.

Nel centro di Boston, dietro la facciata Beaux-Arts datata 1903, si cela una perfetta combinazione fra un servizio ineguagliabile e l'intimità di una residenza privata. Su un totale di dieci piani sono suddivisi 60 appartamenti e suite, dotati di tutti i comfort immaginabili. La cantina ospita oltre ai vini anche il ristorante dell'hotel, nel quale insieme a vini eccezionali si servono specialità della casa impreziosite dalle erbe aromatiche coltivate nel giardino sul tetto dell'edificio.

The address is Fifteen Beacon Street, the flair is all Boston.

An der Fifteen Beacon gelegen, lebt das Hotel vom Bostoner Flair.

Situé sur la Fifteen Beacon, l'hôtel vit du charme de Boston.

Situado en la Fifteen Beacon, el hotel se nutre del ambiente bostoniano.

Ubicato sulla Fifteen Beacon, l'hotel vive del fascino della città di Boston.

Restrained colors set the tone in the two-room suites.

Die Zwei-Raum-Suiten: Ihre Atmosphäre wird vor allem durch die gedeckten Töne bestimmt.

Les suites à deux pièces : leur atmosphère est principalement déterminée par des tons neutres.

En las suites de dos habitaciones el ambiente está definido por los tonos apagados.

Nelle suite bilocali predominano le tonalità cromatiche neutre.

Four Seasons Hotel New York

New York, New York

A grandiose skyscraper and a unique cosmopolitan hang-out between Park and Madison Avenue. The design by IM Pei and Frank Williams reinterprets the style of New York's legendary grand hotels from the 1920s. In the bar and restaurant, the clientele is about as exclusive as it gets—Hollywood stars mingle with Wall Street bankers and Park Avenue princesses. The hotel's 368 rooms are spread across 52 floors, with the upper levels enjoying unrivalled views of Central Park.

Ein grandioser Wolkenkratzer und ein einzigartiger kosmopolitischer Treffpunkt. Zwischen Park und Madison Avenue haben IM Pei und Frank Williams ein Hotel geschaffen, das den Stil der legendären New Yorker Grand-Hotels der 20er Jahre neu interpretiert. Die Zusammensetzung des Publikums in Bar und Restaurant ist an Exklusivität kaum zu übertreffen, Westküsten-Celebrities treffen hier auf Wallstreet-Banker und Park-Avenue-Prinzessinnen. Auf 52 Etagen verteilen sich 368 Zimmer, die oberen haben einen unvergleichlichen Blick auf den Central Park.

Un gratte-ciel grandiose et un rendez-vous cosmopolite unique. IM Pei et Frank Williams ont créé un hôtel entre Park et Madison Avenue qui fournit une nouvelle interprétation du style des grands hôtels légendaires des années 1920. Le rapprochement du public dans le bar et le restaurant ne manque pas d'exclusivité, les célébrités de la côte ouest rencontrent ici les banquiers de Wallstreet et les princesses de Park Avenue. 368 chambres sont réparties sur 52 étages, les chambres du dernier étage ont une vue imprenable sur Central Park.

Un grandioso rascacielos y un punto de encuentro único y cosmopolita. IM Pei y Frank Williams crearon entre Park y Madison Avenue un hotel que interpreta de forma novedosa el estilo legendario de los grandes hoteles neoyorquinos de los años 20. En el bar y restaurante se da cita el público más exclusivo de celebridades de la costa oeste, banqueros de Wallstreet y princesas de la Park Avenue. Las 368 habitaciones del hotel se distribuyen en 52 pisos; las de la parte superior ofrecen inolvidables vistas al Central Park.

Un maestoso grattacielo nonché un luogo d'incontro singolare e cosmopolita. Con il Four Seasons Hotel New York, situato fra Park e Madison Avenue, IM Pei e Frank Williams hanno dato vita ad un'interpretazione, in chiave contemporanea, dello stile dei leggendari Grand Hotel di New York degli anni 1920. Ineguagliabile per esclusività la composizione variegata degli assidui frequentatori di locale notturno e ristorante: dalle celebrità della West Coast ai banchieri di Wall Street o ancora alle debuttanti dell'alta società 368 stanze sono disposte su 52 piani, ai piani superiori con vista incomparabile su Central Park.

The interior design is dominated by a honey-colored sandstone, which IM Pei also used for the Louvre extension in Paris.

Im Innern dominiert der honigfarbene Sandstein, den IM Pei auch für den Louvre-Anbau in Paris verwendete.

À l'intérieur, c'est le grès couleur miel, également utilisé par IM Pei pour l'agrandissement du Louvre à Paris, qui est dominant.

En el interior domina la arenisca del color miel, la misma que IM Pei utilizara para la ampliación del Louvre en París.

All'interno predomina la pietra arenaria color miele utilizzata da IM Pei anche per l'ampliamento del Louvre a Parigi.

Relax and unwind next to the busy lobby in the lounge or the seating areas in front of the huge fireplace. The Art deco accents are clear for all to see.

Neben dem belebten Foyer bieten die Lounge sowie Plätze vor dem überdimensionierten Kamin die Möglichkeit zum Rückzug. Die Anklänge an die Formen des Art déco sind unübersehbar.

Parallèlement au foyer animé, la lounge et l'espace disponible devant la cheminée surdimensionnée permettent de se retirer. Les réminiscences des formes du style Art déco sont évidentes.

Junto al animado vestíbulo, el lounge y el entorno a la gran chimenea invitan al recogimiento. Las semejanzas con las formas del art déco saltan a la vista.

Oltre che nell'animato foyer è possibile ritirarsi in un angolo più tranquillo prendendo posto nella lounge o davanti al camino gigante. Numerosissime le reminiscenze estetiche dell'art déco.

The oversized windows in the rooms and suites provide stunning unobscured views of Central Park and the New York skyline.

Die übergroßen Fenster in den Zimmern und Suiten gewährleisten einen ungestörten, fantastischen Blick auf den Central Park oder die Skyline der Stadt.

Les fenêtres surdimensionnées des chambres et des suites garantissent une vue tranquille et fantastique sur le Central Park ou la silhouette urbaine de la ville.

Los grandes ventanales en las habitaciones y suites garantizan fantásticas claras vistas al Central Park y el conjunto de la ciudad.

Attraverso le enormi finestre di stanze e suite è possibile godere di una fantastica ed indisturbata vista su Central Park o sullo skyline della città.

Mandarin Oriental, New York

New York, New York

The exclusive development between the 35th and 54th floor of the Time Warner Center is a prestigious address in the heart of Manhattan, with floor-to-ceiling windows that offer paramount views overlooking the city. This luxury hotel with 248 rooms and suites provides a stunning blend of modern interiors with Art deco style furnishings and elegant Asian-influenced design. Ornate kimonos decorate the walls, and contemporary art, notably two modern sculptures by Dale Chihuly.

Das Hotel befindet sich zwischen Etage 35 und 54 des Time Warner Centers, einer Prestige-Adresse im Herzen Manhattans. Die raumhohen Fenster bieten einen überragenden Ausblick auf die Metropole. In den 248 luxuriösen Zimmern und Suiten findet der Gast einen Mix aus moderner Einrichtung, Möbeln im Art-déco-Stil und elegantem, asiatisch inspirierten Design. Verzierte Kimonos schmücken die Wände. Ein besonderer Blickfang ist die zeitgenössische Kunst. Zu den Highlights gehören zwei Glasskulpturen von Dale Chihuly.

L'hôtel se trouve entre le 35ème et le 54ème étage du Time Warner Center, une adresse prestigieuse au cœur de Manhattan. Les fenêtres du sol au plafond offrent une vue surplombant la métropole. Dans les 248 chambres et suites de luxe, l'hôte découvre un aménagement moderne, associant des meubles de style Art déco et un design élégant d'inspiration asiatique. Des kimonos ouvrés décorent les murs. L'art contemporain attire particulièrement les regards. Les points forts en sont deux sculptures de verre de Dale Chihuly.

El hotel ocupa las plantas 35 a 54 del Time Warner Center, un de los sitios más prestigiosos en el corazón de Manhattan. Los altos ventanales presentan una insuperable vista sobre la metrópoli. Las 248 lujosas habitaciones y suites ofrecen al huésped una fusión entre decoración moderna, mobiliario de estilo art déco y elegante diseño de inspiración asiática. Adornados quimonos decoran las paredes. Las piezas de arte contemporáneo son el centro de todas las miradas. Entre las piezas más destacadas se encuentran dos esculturas de cristal de Dale Chihuly.

L'hotel si trova tra il 35° e il 54° piano del Time Warner Center, un prestigioso indirizzo nel cuore di Manhattan. Dalle finestre extradimensionate alte fino al soffitto, si gode una magnifica vista sulla metropoli. L'arredamento delle 248 lussuose camere e suite combina elementi moderni, mobili in stile art déco ed elegante design di ispirazione asiatica. Alle pareti sono appesi kimono riccamente lavorati. Di particolare interesse è l'arte contemporanea: tra i pezzi più prestigiosi ci sono due sculture in vetro di Dale Chihuly.

The city's most dramatic 75-foot lap pool with a window wall that frames lofty views over the Midtown Manhattan and the Hudson River.

Der Pool mit der besten Aussicht der Stadt: Die Glaswand neben dem 23 Meter langen Becken gibt den Blick auf Midtown Manhattan, den Central Park und den Hudson River frei.

La piscine ayant la meilleure vue de la ville : la paroi de verre le long des 23 mètres du bassin ouvre le panorama sur Midtown Manhattan, Central Park et la rivière Hudson.

La piscina brinda la mejor vista sobre la ciudad: La pared de cristal junto a la piscina de 23 metros de largo ofrece un panorama sobre Midtown Manhattan, el Central Park y el Hudson River.

La piscina con la vista più bella della città: la parete di vetro posta accanto alla vasca, lunga 23 metri, regala la vista su Midtown Manhattan, il Central Park e il fiume Hudson.

The marble bathrooms are larger than some NewYork apartments and have stunning views of Central Park and the city skyline.

Die Marmorbadezimmer sind größer als so manches New Yorker Apartment. Sie bieten außerdem eine fantastische Aussicht auf den Central Park und die Skyline.

Les salles de bain en marbre sont plus grandes que nombre d'appartements new-yorkais. Elles offrent de plus une vue fantastique sur Central Park et la silhouette urbaine.

Los cuartos de baño de mármol superan las dimensiones de algunos apartamentos neoyorquinos. Desde aquí se aprecia una fantástica vista al Central Park y al conjunto de la ciudad.

I bagni di marmo sono più grandi di alcuni appartamenti newyorkesi. Da essi si gode inoltre la fantastica vista del Central Park e dello skyline.

Hotel (The Mercer)
New York, New York

An engaging, glamorous SoHo hangout with a hint of Bohemia housed in a splendid Romanesque revival building. All 75 guest rooms have the minimalist design of a New York City loft, with exposed brickwork, bare wooden floors, industry size windows, and floor-to-ceiling iron support columns. The rooms are decorated with pale leather screens and banquettes, low oval coffee tables on antique Turkish carpets, dark African woods and custom-designed Christian Liaigre furniture upholstered in natural fibers.

Dieser glamouröse SoHo-Treffpunkt mit einem Hauch Boheme befindet sich in einem prächtigen Gebäude im romanischen Stil. Alle 75 Zimmer weisen das minimalistische Design einer New Yorker Loftwohnung auf. Charakteristisch dafür sind freiliegendes Mauerwerk, nackte Holzböden, riesige Fenster und eiserne Stützpfeiler. Die Räume sind mit hellen, ledernen Lampenschirmen, niedrigen ovalen Beistelltischen, antiken türkischen Teppichen und dunklen afrikanischen Hölzern eingerichtet. Die extra angefertigten Möbel von Christian Liaigre wurden mit natürlichen Stoffen gepolstert.

Ce point de rencontre glamoureux de SoHo, légèrement bohème, se trouve dans un somptueux bâtiment de style romain. Les 75 chambres présentent toutes le design minimaliste d'un loft new-yorkais. Celui-ci se caractérise par une maçonnerie dégagée, des planchers en bois nu, d'immenses baies vitrées et des piliers de fer. Les pièces sont aménagées avec des abat-jour en cuir clair, des dessertes ovales basses, des tapis turcs antiques et des bois africains sombres. Les meubles, dessinés par Christian Liaigre et fabriqués spécialement, ont été rembourrés de tissus de fibres naturelles.

Este glamouroso punto de encuentro en el SoHo con aire bohemio ocupa un magnífico edificio de estilo románico. Las 75 habitaciones presentan el diseño minimalista de un loft neoyorquino. Son característicos los suelos de madera sin tratar, la mampostería descubierta, amplios ventanales y pilares de apoyo en hierro. Las habitaciones están decoradas con claras pantallas de lámpara de piel, mesas auxiliares bajas y ovaladas, antiguas alfombras turcas y maderas africanas oscuras. Los muebles de diseño exclusivo de Christian Liagre han sido tapizados con telas naturales.

Questo prestigioso luogo d'incontro di SoHo, dal fascino un po' bohémien, si trova in uno splendido edificio di stile romanico. Tutte le 75 camere sono realizzate nel design minimalista di una loft newyorkese, con i caratteristici muri a vista, parquet, grandi vetrate e colonne di ferro. Le camere sono arredate con lampade di pelle chiara, tavolini ovali, antichi tappeti turchi e legni scuri africani. I mobili Christian Liaigre, confezionati su misura, sono imbottiti con fibre naturali.

The serene lobby has an unmarked reception desk and a wood-paneled library full of books for guests. Furnishings are spare, since the beauty of a place lays in its empty spaces.

In der ruhigen Lobby befinden sich eine unaufdringliche Rezeption sowie eine holzgetäfelte Gästebibliothek. Die Möblierung des gesamten Hauses ist sparsam. Die Schönheit liegt in den Freiräumen.

Dans le salon tranquille, la réception se fait discrète ; on y trouve également une bibliothèque pour les hôtes, lambrissée de bois. L'ameublement de tout l'établissement est parcimonieux. La beauté réside dans les espaces libres.

El apacible lobby alberga la discreta recepción y una biblioteca para los huéspedes revestida de madera. La casa se destaca por lo sobrio del mobiliario. La belleza se aprecia en los espacios abiertos.

Nella tranquilla lobby si trovano una reception estremamente discreta e una biblioteca rivestita con pannelli di legno, destinata agli ospiti. L'intero hotel è arredato spartanamente: il fascino è tutto negli spazi vuoti.

The almost decadent two-person marble tubs, some surrounded by mirrors, open up to the rustic decor of the minimalistic bedroom.

Die fast dekadenten Marmorbadewannen für zwei Personen, einige sind von Spiegeln umgeben, liegen ohne weitere Abtrennung neben den minimalistisch dekorierten Schlafzimmern.

Les baignoires de marbre pour deux personnes, presque décadentes, certaines d'entre elles sont entourées de miroirs, jouxtent sans cloison les chambres à coucher au décor minimaliste.

Las refinadas bañeras de mármol para dos personas, algunas rodeadas de espejos, están dispuestas sin separación alguna junto a las habitaciones de decoración minimalista.

Le vasche da bagno di marmo per due persone sono di gusto quasi decadente, alcune sono circondate da specchi. Si trovano accanto alle camere da letto, decorate con gusto minimalista, senza alcuna parete divisoria.

Plaza Athénée

New York, New York

This decadent, European-style hotel is a rarified gem tucked away on a quiet side street on the fashionable Upper East Side of Manhattan. The lobby is a crystal-and-marble fantasy, with stunning floral arrangements, opulent chandeliers, ornate mirrors, and richly hued murals. The 149 guest rooms and suites have Portuguese marble bathrooms, tapestry-covered pillows, hand-painted silk draperies, and marble-floored foyers that give them a real residential feel.

Dieses opulente Hotel im europäischen Stil gleicht einem seltenen Edelstein. Es liegt versteckt in einer ruhigen Seitenstraße auf der begehrten Upper East Side von Manhattan. Die Lobby ist eine kristallene und marmorne Fantasie mit überwältigenden Blumenarrangements, ausladenden Kronleuchtern, verzierten Spiegeln und leuchtenden Wandgemälden. Zu den 149 Zimmern gehören Bäder aus portugiesischem Marmor, Gobelin-Kissen, handbemalte Seidenstoffe und ein Foyer mit Marmorboden, das für eine villenartige Note sorgt.

Cet hôtel opulent de style européen ressemble à une pierre précieuse rare. Il se cache dans une rue latérale tranquille dans le très recherché Upper East Side de Manhattan. Le salon est une composition originale de marbre et de cristal, avec de sublimes arrangements floraux, des lustres en encorbellement, des miroirs ornés et des peintures murales lumineuses. Les 149 chambres et suites possèdent des salles de bain en marbre portugais, des coussins en tapisserie des Gobelins, des soieries peintes à la main. Le sol en marbre du hall d'entrée apporte une note princière.

Este opulento hotel de estilo europeo se asemeja a una rara piedra preciosa. Se encuentra situado en una tranquila calle en la codiciada Upper East Side de Manhattan. El lobby es una fantasía de cristal y mármol con impresionantes arreglos florales, grandiosas arañas de cristal, espejos decorados y deslumbrantes murales. Las 149 habitaciones habitaciones y suites cuentan con cuartos de baño de mármol portugués, cojines de tapiz, sedas pintadas a mano y un vestíbulo con suelo de mármol que aporta un aire señorial.

Questo opulento hotel in stile europeo è un vero gioiello nascosto in una tranquilla strada laterale della frequentatissima Upper East Side di Manhattan. La lobby è una fantasia di cristallo e marmo, impreziosita da magnifiche composizioni floreali, lampadari di cristallo, specchi decorati e luminosi dipinti. Le 149 camere e suite dispongono di bagni di marmo portoghese, cuscini di gobelin, stoffe di seta dipinte a mano e di un foyer dal pavimento di marmo che conferisce all'ambiente un tocco signorile.

This little jewel box of a hotel is located just steps from the chic boutiques of Fifth Avenue and the city's finest restaurants.

Dieses kleine Juwel von einem Hotel liegt nur wenige Schritte von den schicken Boutiquen der Fifth Avenue und den besten Restaurants der Stadt entfernt.

Ce petit joyau d'hôtel n'est qu'à quelques pas des magasins chic de la Fifth Avenue et des meilleurs restaurants de la ville.

Esta perla de hotel está ubicada a poco pasos de las elegantes boutiques de la Fifth Avenue y de los mejores restaurantes de la ciudad.

Un hotel che è un piccolo gioiello: a pochi passi dalle eleganti boutique della Fifth Avenue e dai migliori ristoranti della città.

With its plush velvet cushions, hand-painted murals, chiffon-colored walls, and Italian marble floors, the Plaza Athénée has a distinctly European ambience.

Mit seinen plüschigen Samtkissen, den handgemalten Wandgemälden, den hellen Wänden und Böden aus italienischem Marmor hat das Plaza Athénée ganz klar eine europäische Atmosphäre.

Avec ses coussins de velours moelleux, les tableaux muraux peints à la main, les murs clairs et les sols de marbre italien, le Plaza Athénée dégage incontestablement une atmosphère européenne.

Sus suaves cojines de terciopelo, los murales pintados a mano, las paredes claras y los suelos de mármol italiano confieren al Plaza Athénée un indiscutible ambiente europeo.

Morbidi cuscini di velluto, dipinti, pareti e pavimenti di marmo italiano: al Plaza Athénée prevale un gusto spiccatamente europeo.

The Lowell

New York, New York

Located on a quiet, tree-lined residential street, the Lowell epitomizes "old New York" luxury. The suites have all of the civilized comforts of home, replete with stocked bookshelves, gilt-framed paintings and plush armchairs and sofas. All 70 deluxe rooms and suites are individually decorated with lush carpets, fine antiques, and such ornamental accents as Chinese porcelain bowls, bronze figurines and botanical prints.

An einer ruhigen, baumgesäumten Wohnstraße gelegen, verkörpert das Lowell alteingesessenen New Yorker Luxus. Selbstverständlich fehlt keine Annehmlichkeit, die der Gast von Zuhause gewöhnt ist. Gut gefüllte Bücherregale gehören genauso dazu, wie goldgerahmte Bilder und plüschige Sessel und Sofas. Alle 70 Deluxe-Zimmer und Suiten sind individuell mit dicken Teppichen und edlen Antiquitäten versehen. Chinesische Porzellanschalen, Bronzefiguren und botanische Drucke setzen Akzente.

Situé dans une rue résidentielle tranquille bordée d'arbres, le Lowell incarne le luxe new-yorkais bien établi. L'hôte dispose bien sûr de toutes les commodités auxquelles il est habitué chez lui : des étagères garnies de livres, des tableaux aux cadres dorés et des fauteuils et canapés moelleux. Les 70 chambres et suite Deluxe sont dotées chacune d'un épais tapis et d'objets antiques individuellement sélectionnés. Des coupes de porcelaine chinoise, des statuettes de bronze et des gravures à sujets botaniques complètent la décoration.

En una calle tranquila flanqueada por árboles está situado el Lowell, hotel que encarna el más arraigado lujo neoyorquino. Como era de esperar, aquí el huésped no echa de menos ninguna de las comodidades que querría en su propia casa. Una muy bien surtida biblioteca, cuadros con marcos de oro, confortables sillones y sofás configuran el ambiente. Las 70 habitaciones y suites "deluxe" cuentan con una decoración individual con gruesas alfombras y valiosas antigüedades. Fuentes de porcelana china, figuras de bronce y grabados con motivos botánicos imponen a la estancia un exquisito carácter.

Situato in una strada residenziale tranquilla e alberata, il Lowell è sinonimo di autentico lusso newyorkese. Ovviamente non manca nessuna delle comodità cui l'ospite è abituato a casa propria, come una biblioteca ben fornita, quadri dalle cornici dorate e comode poltrone e divani. Tutte le 70 camere e suite deluxe sono arredate in modo individuale, con soffici tappeti e pregiati pezzi d'antiquariato. Porcellane cinesi, figure di bronzo e stampe floreali conferiscono un tocco di eleganza.

The rooms and suites are adorned with beautiful antique furniture and prints, rich chintzes, satins, and other rich floral fabrics. Large desks and engulfing comforters make you feel at home.

In den Zimmern und Suiten wohnt der Gast inmitten wunderschöner antiker Möbel und Drucke. Üppige, prächtige Stoffe mit floralen Mustern sorgen zusammen mit großen Schreibtischen und kuscheligen Bettdecken für eine anheimelnde Atmosphäre.

Dans les chambres et suites, l'hôte séjourne au milieu de meubles antiques et de magnifiques gravures. De splendides étoffes aux motifs floraux exubérants, de grands bureaux et de couvre-lits douillets créent une atmosphère confortable.

En las habitaciones y suites el huésped vive en medio de bellísimos muebles antiguos y grabados. Telas de texturas opulentas con motivos florales junto con grandes escritorios y cálidos edredones crean un ambiente hogareño.

Nelle camere e suite l'ospite vive tra magnifici mobili e stampe d'epoca. Stoffe pesanti e pregiate a motivi floreali, scrivanie massicce e soffici coperte creano un ambiente caldo e familiare.

Wood-burning fireplaces, *a rarity for New York City hotels, are lined with bookshelves, and almost all of the 47 individually decorated suites have fully equipped kitchens.*

In den *von Bücherregalen umrahmten Kaminen brennen echte Holzscheite, eine Seltenheit in New Yorker Hotels. Fast jede der 47 individuell dekorierten Suiten hat eine voll ausgestattete Küche.*

Dans les *cheminées flanquées de rayonnages brûlent de vraies bûches, une rareté dans les hôtels new-yorkais. Presque toutes les suites sur les 47 décorées différemment possèdent une cuisine entièrement équipée.*

En las *chimeneas rodeadas de libros arden auténticos haces de leña, algo inusual en los hoteles neoyorquinos. De las 47 suites, casi todas están decoradas individualmente y poseen una cocina completamente equipada.*

Nei camini *posti tra gli scaffali pieni di libri bruciano veri ciocchi di legno, una rarità in un hotel newyorkese. Quasi tutte le 47 suite arredate con gusto individuale dispongono di una cucina modernamente attrezzata.*

Four Seasons Resort Great Exuma

Emerald Bay, Bahamas

The ocean takes center stage at this hotel. Guests have exclusive access to a great swimming bay with a white sandy beach. All 183 rooms offer views of Emerald Bay, while the hotel golf course stretches along the coast over sand dunes and protected mangrove fields to a rocky peninsula. The spa offers relaxing massages under the open sky, using island herbs, flowers, oils and locally sourced natural salts.

Das Meer ist das zentrale Thema dieses Hotels. Den Gästen steht eine private Badebucht mit weißem Sandstrand zur Verfügung. Alle 183 Zimmer bieten einen Blick auf die Emerald Bay. Der hauseigene Golfplatz führt entlang der Küste über Dünenlandschaften und Mangroven-Schutzgebiete bis zu einer felsigen Halbinsel. Im Spa kann man Massagen unter freiem Himmel genießen, bei denen Natursalze aus örtlichen Vorkommen, heimische Kräuter, Blüten und Öle den Körper entspannen.

La mer est le thème central de cet hôtel. Les visiteurs bénéficient d'une baie privée destinée à la baignade, avec une plage de sable blanc. Les 183 chambres offrent une vue superbe sur la Emerald Bay. Le terrain de golf de l'hôtel longe la côte et traverse les paysages des dunes et les réserves des mangroves pour atteindre une presqu'île rocheuse. Dans le spa, on peut profiter de massages en plein air, au cours desquels les sels naturels provenants de gisements locaux, les plantes, les fleurs et les huiles locales sont utilisés pour détendre le corps.

El mar es el tema principal de este hotel. Los huéspedes tienen a su disposición una bahía privada con playas de arena blanca. Las 183 habitaciones se asoman a la Emerald Bay. El campo de golf, de propiedad del hotel, se extiende a lo largo de la costa a través de un paisaje de dunas y una reserva de manglares que alcanza una península rocosa. En el spa se puede disfrutar de masajes al aire libre con sustancias relajantes como sales naturales, hierbas, flores y aceites autóctonos.

Il mare è il tema centrale di questo hotel, a cominciare dalla baia privata con spiaggia di sabbia bianchissima a disposizione degli ospiti. Da tutte le 183 stanze si può ammirare l'Emerald Bay. Il campo da golf privato si snoda lungo la riva costeggiando dune ed aree protette a vegetazione di mangrovie fino ad arrivare ad una penisola rocciosa. La Spa propone massaggi a cielo aperto, il cui effetto rilassante per il corpo è potenziato dall'uso di sali naturali ricavati da giacimenti del luogo nonché erbe, fiori ed oli locali.

The atmospheric hotel pool is perfect for a daytime or evening dip.

Der Pool ist sowohl am Tage als auch in der Nacht ein stimmungsvoller Ort.

De jour comme de nuit, la piscine est un lieu évocateur.

La piscina es tanto de día como de noche un rincón cargado de ambiente.

La piscina è un luogo ricco di atmosfera tanto di giorno quanto di notte.

Colonial architecture sits in harmony with contemporary beach resort flair.

Der Stil der Kolonialzeit vermischt sich hier mit dem Strand- und Badeflair der heutigen Zeit.

Le style de l'époque coloniale se confond ici avec le charme de la plage et de la baignade de l'époque actuelle.

El estilo de la época colonial se mezcla aquí con el ambiente de playa actual.

Lo stile dell'epoca coloniale si mescola al fascino della vita da mare dell'epoca contemporanea.

One&Only Ocean Club

Paradise Island, Bahamas

Situated amid rolling hills and decorated with classical statues of bronze and marble, this paradise on earth was modeled on the verdant gardens of the Palace of Versailles. Fascinating arches from the imported ruins of a 12th century Augustinian monastery are found at the resort's highest point, while hibiscus and bougainvillea line the path from the terraced garden down to the beach. Mahogany beds, parquet floors and sisal rugs in the rooms and suites create an atmosphere that is elegant and yet comfortably informal.

Das Paradies auf Erden wurde nach dem Vorbild der Grünanlagen des Schlosses von Versailles in einer hügeligen Landschaft angelegt und mit europäischen Bronze- und Marmorstatuen dekoriert. An der höchsten Stelle erheben sich die beeindruckenden Bögen der importierten Ruine eines Augustinerklosters aus dem 12. Jahrhundert. Hibiskus- und Bougainvilleasträucher säumen den Weg vom Strand hinauf zum Terrassengarten. In den Zimmern und Suiten sorgen Mahagonibetten, Parkettböden und Sisalteppiche für die richtige Mischung aus Eleganz und Lässigkeit.

Le paradis sur terre a été aménagé selon le modèle des jardins du château de Versailles dans un paysage vallonné et décoré avec des statues européennes en bronze et en marbre. Sur le point le plus élevé s'élèvent les arcs impressionnants de la ruine importée d'un cloître augustin du 12ème siècle. Les hibiscus et les bougainvillées bordent le chemin qui mène de la plage au jardin en terrasse. Dans les chambres et les suites, les lits en acajou, le parquet et les tapis en sisal créent une association parfaite d'élégance et de nonchalance.

Este paraíso terrenal fue creado en un paisaje de colinas, siguiendo el modelo de los jardines de Versalles y decorado con estatuas europeas de bronce y mármol. En la parte más elevada se levantan los impresionantes arcos de las ruinas importadas de un monasterio agustino del siglo XII. Los arbustos de hibiscos y buganvillas acordonan el camino que conduce de la playa hasta el jardín de la terraza. Camas de madera mahagoni, suelos de parqué y alfombras de sisal visten las habitaciones de elegancia y sencillez.

Il paradiso in terra è stato creato in una zona collinare su modello dei giardini del castello di Versailles e decorato con statue europee in bronzo e marmo. Sul punto più elevato si ergono gli archi imponenti delle rovine di un chiostro agostiniano del XII secolo. Cespugli di ibisco e bouganville fiancheggiano il sentiero che dalla spiaggia sale su per il giardino a terrazze. Nelle stanze e nelle suite, la giusta combinazione fra eleganza ed informalità è dettata dalla scelta di letti in mogano, pavimenti in parquet e tappeti di sisal.

Every lovingly designed detail in the rooms and suites was selected with the utmost care.

Jedes Detail der Zimmer und Suiten wurde mit viel Liebe ausgesucht und gestaltet.

Chaque détail des chambres et des suites a été choisi et agencé avec beaucoup de soin.

Cada detalle de las habitaciones y suites ha sido seleccionado y dispuesto con todo el esmero.

Ogni dettaglio nelle stanze e nelle suite è stato scelto e realizzato con estrema cura.

The hotel gardens are a visual treat for anyone with green-fingered leanings.

Die Gartenanlage ist ein Fest für die Augen eines jeden Pflanzenliebhabers.

Le jardin est un régal pour les yeux de tous les amoureux des plantes.

Los jardines son una verdadera fiesta para los amantes de la vegetación.

I giardini sono una delizia agli occhi di tutti gli appassionati di botanica.

St. Regis Temenos Villas
Anguilla, British West Indies

This luxury resort on the island of Anguilla consists of a trio of dazzling white villas, with architecture and furnishings inspired by the sea, sand and sky. Each secluded island hideaway boasts four master suites, a private pool and a jacuzzi overlooking the ocean. The open-air pavilion restaurant is ideal for romantic dining. On request, the head chef can prepare food on the beach, or even cook for you in your villa. Guests can also enjoy freshly prepared cocktails at the beach bar hut.

Die auf der Insel Anguilla gelegene Villenanlage besteht aus drei blendend weißen Villen, deren Architektur und Einrichtung ganz von den Themen Meer, Sand und Himmel inspiriert sind. Jede dieser abgeschiedenen Inseloasen umfasst vier Master-Suiten, einen eigenen Pool und einen Whirlpool mit Blick auf den Ozean. Ein Freiluftpavillon dient als Restaurant für romantisches Speisen. Auf Wunsch serviert der Chefkoch am Strand oder kocht direkt in der Villa. Am Strand selbst findet der Gast ein Strandhäuschen, in welchem frische Drinks angeboten werden.

Le complexe construit sur l'île d'Anguilla compte trois villas parfaitement blanches dont l'architecture et l'aménagement empruntent tout aux thèmes de la mer, de la plage et du ciel. Chaque oasis insulaire isolé comprend quatre Master Suites, sa propre piscine et un jacuzzi avec vue sur l'océan. Un pavillon en plein air sert de restaurant pour les dîners romantiques. Sur demande, le chef cuisinier sert sur la plage ou cuisine directement dans la villa. Sur la plage même, le visiteur trouvera aussi une cabane de plage dans laquelle des boissons fraîches lui seront proposées.

El conjunto de villas situado en la isla Anguilla está compuesto por tres magníficas villas blancas, cuya arquitectura y decoración se inspiran en tres temas: mar, arena y cielo. Cada uno de estos oasis comprende cuatro master suites una piscina propia y un jacuzzi con vistas al océano. Un pabellón al aire libre hace funciones de restaurante para comidas románticas. A petición, el jefe cocinero sirve en la playa o directamente en la villa. En la playa, los huéspedes disponen de cabañas en las que se ofrecen bebidas refrescantes.

Ubicato sull'isola Anguilla, il resort è costituito da tre bianchissime ville interamente ispirate, tanto per l'architettura quanto per l'arredamento, ai temi mare, sabbia e cielo. Ognuna delle tre oasi isolate comprende quattro master suite, una piscina ed una vasca idromassaggio con vista sull'oceano. Un gazebo all'aperto funge da ristorante per cene romantiche. A richiesta, lo chef serve le sue specialità sulla spiaggia o le cucina direttamente in villa. Sulla spiaggia, un cocktail bar accoglie gli ospiti con le sue proposte rinfrescanti.

The resort's three villas are set amidst rocky scenery and flowering plantlife.

Inmitten von Felsen und blühender Pflanzenwelt liegen die einzelnen Villen dieser Anlage.

C'est au milieu des rochers et du monde végétal florissant que les différentes villas de ce complexe ont été construites.

Las villas están insertadas entre rocas y una flora exuberante.

Le tre ville, indipendenti l'una dall'altra, sono contornate da scogli e da una flora rigogliosa.

Each captivating villa has a clear, bright design. Suites are appointed with carefully selected furnishings and artworks.

Jede Villa besticht durch eine klare, helle Gestaltung. Die Suiten sind mit ausgewählten Möbelstücken und Kunstobjekten eingerichtet.

Chaque villa séduit par la précision et la clarté de son aménagement. Les suites sont aménagées avec des meubles et des objets d'art choisis.

Cada una de las villas emana un interior claro y luminoso. Las suites han sido decoradas con un mobiliario seleccionado y piezas de arte.

Ognuna villa si contraddistingue per l'arredamento sobrio e luminoso, impreziosito da mobili e oggetti d'arte scelti con cura.

Carlisle Bay

Antigua, British West Indies

Located on a secluded beach with a backdrop of rainforests and lush landscaping, the resort daringly eschews everything colonial by designing subdued basic interiors to draw attention to the captivating colors of the blooming exotic gardens. Serene minimalistic interiors are combined with the Japanese decorative ideal of perfection, with white walls and weathered wood. For that extra urban touch, there are in-room espresso machines, a pool with semi-submerged sun loungers, and a 45-seat cinema.

An einem abgeschiedenen Strand liegt dieser Zufluchtsort inmitten des Regenwaldes. Koloniale Reminiszenzen sucht der Gast hier vergebens. Die zurückhaltende Einrichtung lenkt den Blick auf die leuchtenden Farben des exotischen Gartens. Der minimalistische Stil strebt ein perfektionistisch-japanisches Designideal an. Dazu gehören weiße Wände und verwittertes Holz. Für den extra-urbanen Touch gibt es auf jedem Zimmer eine Espressomaschine, einen Pool mit vom Wasser umspülten Sonnenliegen und ein Kino mit 45 Plätzen.

Au bord d'une plage isolée, ce refuge se niche au cœur de la forêt tropicale. L'hôte cherchera en vain des réminiscences coloniales. La décoration discrète oriente les regards vers les couleurs lumineuses du jardin exotique. Le style minimaliste tend vers un idéal de design japonais perfectionniste, incarné par la blancheur des murs et l'effritement du bois. Pour l'indispensable touche d'urbanité, il y a une machine à espresso dans chaque chambre, une piscine avec des chaises longues, les pieds dans l'eau, et un cinéma de 45 places.

En una playa aislada se ubica este refugio en medio de la selva tropical. Resulta en vano buscar aquí reminiscencias coloniales. La sobria decoración encauza la mirada hacia los luminosos colores del exótico jardín. El estilo minimalista se orienta hacía el ideal perfeccionista del diseño japonés, del que hacen parte blancas paredes y madera envejecida. El toque urbano lo imponen las máquinas de café expreso en cada habitación, una piscina con tumbonas bañadas por el agua y un cine con 45 butacas.

Questo ritiro in mezzo alla foresta pluviale è situato su una spiaggia appartata. Nulla ricorda il passato coloniale: l'arredamento discreto richiama l'attenzione sui colori brillanti del giardino esotico. Lo stile minimalista utilizza pareti bianche e legno grezzo, ispirandosi all'ideale perfezionista del design giapponese. Un tocco "cittadino" è dato dalla macchina per l'espresso di cui è provvista ogni stanza, dalla piscina con le brandine immerse nell'acqua e da un cinema con 45 posti.

80 suites have a private sundeck that overlooks stunning views, complete with a hardwood Asian daybed and fluttering voile curtains for added privacy.

Die 80 Suiten haben eine private Sonnenterrasse mit traumhafter Aussicht, die sich am besten vom Tagesbett aus genießen lässt. Voile-Vorhänge schützen vor ungewollten Einblicken.

Les 80 suites disposent d'une terrasse privée au soleil avec une vue merveilleuse dont on profite au mieux en s'installant dans le canapé-lit. Des rideaux de voile protègent des regards indiscrets.

Las 80 suites disponen de una terraza solariega privada provista de tumbonas, ideales para disfrutar de las vistas de ensueño. Las cortinas de muselina otorgan privacidad.

Le 80 suite dispongono di una terrazza privata con una magnifica vista dalle comode brandine. Tende di voile proteggono da sguardi indiscreti.

The vast cathedral-style lobby is flanked with discreet tinkling fountains and lily ponds, white-washed rustic wood floors and contemporary wicker furnishings.

Die große, kathedralenartige Lobby mit weiß getünchten, rustikalen Holzböden und zeitgenössischen Korbmöbeln wird von leise plätschernden Springbrunnen und kleinen Lilien-Teichen gesäumt.

Le grand salon aux allures de cathédrale avec son plancher en bois rustique badigeonné de blanc et ses meubles modernes en osier est entouré de fontaines qui gargouillent doucement et de petits bassins remplis de lys d'eau.

El amplio lobby en forma de catedral con rústicos blanqueados suelos de madera y modernos muebles de mimbre están flanqueados por sonoras fuentes y pequeños estanques de lirios.

La grande lobby, simile ad una cattedrale, con rustici pavimenti di legno imbiancato e moderni mobili di vimini, è circondata da fontane zampillanti e da piccoli stagni fioriti di ninfee.

Little Dix Bay
A Rosewood Resort

Virgin Gorda, British Virgin Islands

To visit the Antilles is to see the Caribbean at its best—intimate islands, bays, shimmering seas and powdery white beaches. Little Dix Bay offers all this and more thanks to its elevated location. Built with wood and natural stone, the villas and suites are a joy to behold, and their spacious terraces provide a haven of cool shade. Set into the cliff face, the hotel pool is a real delight, while a trio of restaurants serve colorful Caribbean cuisine with aplomb.

Nach wie vor stehen die Antillen für karibisches Lebensgefühl pur: kleine Inseln, Buchten, glitzerndes Meer und puderweißer Strand. Auch Little Dix Bay bietet diese Ausblicke dank seiner Lage auf einer Anhöhe. Die Suiten und Villen sind geprägt von ihrer Bauweise aus Naturstein und Holz. Ihre großen Terrassen ermöglichen Momente des Rückzugs in den kühlen Schatten. Besonders beeindruckend ist der Pool des Hauses, der in die Felsen integriert wurde. Drei Restaurants erfreuen Augen und Gaumen mit einer karibisch-bunten Küche.

Les Antilles symbolisent toujours la pure joie de vivre des Caraïbes : de petites îles, des baies, la mer scintillante et les plages blanches comme la neige. Située en hauteur, Little Dix Bay offre également ces points de vue. Les suites et les villas ont été construites en pierre naturelle et en bois. Leurs grandes terrasses permettent aux visiteurs de se retirer quelques instants à l'ombre fraîche. Intégrée dans le rocher, la piscine de l'hôtel est particulièrement impressionnante. Les trois restaurants sont un régal pour les yeux et un délice pour le palais avec leur cuisine caribéenne variée.

Desde siempre, las Antillas han representado el más puro estilo de vida caribeño: pequeñas islas, bahías, los destellos del mar y las playas de fina arena blanca. También Little Dix Bay ofrece esa vista desde su privilegiada ubicación en una colina. Las suites y villas están construidas con piedra natural y madera. Sus amplias terrazas invitan a disfrutar de apacibles momentos a la sombra. Especialmente fascinante es la piscina de la casa, integrada en las propias rocas. Tres restaurantes se encargan de deleitar la vista y el paladar con su multicolor cocina caribeña.

Da sempre, le Antille sono sinonimo per eccellenza di gioia di vivere secondo l'interpretazione caraibica: piccole isole, baie, mare luccicante e sabbia color bianco cipria. E questa è la vista che si può ammirare anche da Little Dix Bay grazie alla sua posizione sopraelevata. L'atmosfera ricreata nelle suite e nelle ville del resort sottende la scelta dei materiali: pietra naturale e legno. Sulle grandi terrazze è possibile godere di momenti privati nella frescura dell'ombra. Di grande impatto scenografico la piscina del resort, che sembra scaturire naturalmente dagli scogli. Tre ristoranti deliziano i palati (e non solo) degli ospiti con le proposte della creativa cucina caraibica.

The idyllic resort of Little Dix Bay has attracted relaxation-seekers from all over the world since 1963.

Little Dix Bay empfängt bereits seit 1963 Gäste aus aller Welt, die Entspannung in einem Idyll suchen.

Little Dix Bay accueille depuis 1963 des visiteurs du monde entier recherchant la détente dans un cadre idyllique.

Little Dix Bay recibe desde 1963 huéspedes de todo el mundo que buscan relajarse en un entorno idílico.

Little Dix Bay accoglie già dal 1963 ospiti provenienti da tutto il mondo alla ricerca di una vacanza all'insegna del relax in un contesto idilliaco.

Hotel highlights include spa showers that simulate natural rainfall and a private pool.

Brausen, die einen natürlichen Regenguss simulieren, und ein eigener Pool gehören zu den Extras des Hauses.

Les douches qui simulent une ondée naturelle et la piscine de l'hôtel font partie des avantages offerts par la maison.

Las duchas a modo de lluvia natural y una piscina propia forman parte de los extras de la casa.

I dettagli che fanno la differenza: soffione doccia effetto pioggia e piscina privata.

Cotton House
Mustique, The Grenadines

Mustique is a remarkable and exclusive island in the Grenadines. It is privately owned by a company which presides over a portfolio of 60 luxury villas, an intimate holiday lodge and Cotton House, its one and only hotel. Guests are welcomed in a distinctly British style. Indeed the elegant suites were modeled on designs by celebrated stage architect Oliver Messel. The island's beaches are almost exclusively the domain of the world's rich, powerful and beautiful.

Das zu den Grenadinen zählende Mustique ist ungewöhnlich und exklusiv zugleich. Die Insel ist im Besitz einer Firma, die neben 60 Luxusvillen und einem kleinen Gästehaus auch das Cotton House als einziges Hotel im Portfolio hat. Dort empfängt man die Gäste ausgesprochen britisch. Die exklusive Suiten entstammen den Entwürfen des Designers und Bühnenbildners Oliver Messel. An den Stränden sind die Schönen, Reichen und Prominenten aus aller Welt fast unter sich.

Appartenant aux Grenadines, Moustique est à la fois inhabituelle et exclusive. L'île est administrée par une société qui possède également, parallèlement à 60 villas de luxe et un petit hôtel, un unique complexe hôtelier, le Cotton House. On y accueille les visiteurs de manière très britannique. Les suites exclusives ont été conçues à partir des créations du designer et scénographe Oliver Messel. Sur les plages, les personnes belles, riches et célèbres du monde entier sont quasiment entre elles.

La isla Mustique, parte del archipielago de las Granadinas, es extraordinaria y exclusiva a la vez. Ésta es propiedad de una empresa, que junto a 60 villas de lujo y un pequeño hotel, posee también el Cotton House, el único hotel en su repertorio. Aquí se recibe a los huéspedes con un marcado estilo británico. Las exclusivas suites son obras originales del escenógrafo y diseñador Oliver Messel. Por sus playas pasean bellezas, ricos y personalidades de todo el mundo.

Fra le isole Grenadine di cui fa parte Mustique è la più insolita ed allo stesso tempo esclusiva: di proprietà di un gruppo che annovera nel suo portafoglio come unico hotel, oltre a 60 ville di lusso e ad una piccola foresteria, il Cotton House. Qui agli ospiti viene riservato un trattamento consono alla migliore tradizione britannica. Le suite esclusive sono opera del designer e scenografo Oliver Messel. Le spiagge sono animate quasi esclusivamente dai ricchi, belli e famosi di tutto il mondo.

Romance of nature meets four-poster bed luxury—scattered across the park-like grounds, six lodges and cottages contain 19 rooms and suites.

Naturromantik trifft auf Himmelbett — 19 Suiten und Zimmer sind in sechs Gebäuden und Cottages über das parkartige Gelände verstreut.

Le romantisme naturel est associé au lit à baldaquin — 19 suites et chambres sont réparties dans six bâtiments et cottages sur le terrain aménagé comme un parc.

Fusión entre el romanticismo natural y la cama con dosel — 19 suites y habitaciones repartidas en seis edificios y chalés sobre una amplia área ajardinada.

L'atmosfera romantica all'insegna della natura ben si sposa con i letti a baldacchino delle 19 suite e stanze distribuite in sei edifici e cottage su tutto il resort costruito a mo' di parco.

Tradition meets modernity—wooden verandas and exposed stone walls dovetail with contemporary design and state-of-the-art technology.

Tradition trifft auf Moderne – zur Veranda aus Holz und offenen Steinmauern gesellen sich zeitgenössisches Design und modernste Technik.

La rencontre de la tradition avec le moderne – le design contemporain et une technique de pointe cohabitent avec la véranda en bois et les murs de pierre ouverts.

Donde se abrazan modernidad y tradición – en las terrazas de madera y los muros de piedra abiertos se funden el diseño contemporáneo y la técnica más moderna.

La tradizione ben si sposa con la modernità –verande in legno e muri a vista si coniugano alla perfezione con design contemporaneo e sofisticati accorgimenti tecnici.

Le Sereno

St. Barthélemy, French West Indies, Caribbean

An intimate, elegant beachfront sanctuary with only 37 exquisitely furnished suites that are placed directly on the 600 feet of beach that overlooks the picturesque turquoise cove called Grand Cul-de Sac. The famed Parisian interior designer Christian Liaigre created sleek villas with stylishly minimal taupe and cream furnishings with straight lines, white fabrics, and dark warm woods that evoke a relaxed St. Barths feel.

Mit nur 37 exquisit möblierten Suiten gehört dieses Hotel zu den besonders intimen und eleganten Schmuckstücken. Es liegt direkt an einem etwa 200 Meter langen Strand in der pittoresken, türkisen Grand-Cul-de-Sac-Bucht. Der bekannte Pariser Innenarchitekt Christian Liaigre ist für das Design der eleganten Villen mit ihren minimalistischen Möbeln in Grau und Creme verantwortlich. Gerade Linien, weiße Stoffe und dunkle, warme Hölzer lösen schon beim Betreten das entspannte Gefühl aus, das typisch für St. Barth ist.

Avec seulement 37 suites à l'ameublement exquis, cet hôtel est une perle particulièrement intime et élégante. Il est situé directement au bord d'une plage de 200 mètres dans la pittoresque baie aux eaux turquoise du Grand Cul-de-Sac. Le célèbre architecte d'intérieur parisien Christian Liaigre est responsable de l'agencement des élégantes villas avec leurs meubles minimalistes gris et crème. Des lignes droites, des étoffes blanches et des bois sombres et chauds font ressentir dès l'arrivée l'atmosphère décontractée de St Barth.

Las 37 suites de mobiliario exquisito convierten a este hotel en una íntima y elegante joya. Se encuentra situado directamente en una playa de 200 metros de largo en la pintoresca y turquesa bahía Grand Cul-de Sac. El renombrado arquitecto parisino de interiores Christian Liaigre fue encargado de crear el diseño de las elegantes villas con muebles minimalistas en tonos gris y crema. Líneas rectas, telas blancas y maderas oscuras y cálidas transmiten de inmediato el ambiente relajado de St. Barthélemy.

Con sole 37 suite squisitamente arredate, questo hotel è un gioiello di grande discrezione ed eleganza, situato direttamente su una spiaggia di circa 200 metri nella baia di Grand Cul-de-Sac, pittoresca e turchina. Il design delle eleganti ville, con il loro arredamento minimalista in grigio e crema, è stato ideato dal famoso arredatore parigino Christian Liaigre. Linee diritte, stoffe bianche e legni scuri e caldi danno già al primo sguardo una sensazione di relax tipico di St. Barth.

Oceanfront suites and cottages come with plasma-screen televisions and iPods, private gardens with individual pools, and have access to a cool freshwater pool.

Die am Strand gelegenen Suiten und Häuschen sind alle mit Plasma-Fernseher und iPod ausgestattet. Sie haben einen privaten Garten mit eigenem Pool sowie Zugang zu einem kühlen Süßwasserbecken.

Les suites et bungalows en bord de la plage sont tous équipés de téléviseurs à écran plasma et d'iPods. Ils disposent d'un jardin privé avec une piscine et d'un accès à un bassin d'eau douce fraîche.

Las suites y cabañas, situadas directamente en la playa, están equipadas con televisores de plasma e iPod. Los huéspedes disponen de un jardín privado con piscina propia, así como de acceso a una piscina de fresca agua dulce.

Le suite e le villette situate sulla spiaggia sono provviste di televisore al plasma e iPod. Dispongono di un giardino privato con piscina propria e di un accesso ad una piscina rinfrescata d'acqua dolce.

Le Sereno is like St. Barths itself—a forever fashionable, magical contradiction of simplicity and luxury, and an incredible blend of both modern style and serenity.

Le Sereno ist wie St. Barth – ein zeitlos magischer Kontrast von Simplizität und Luxus mit einer seltenen Kombination von Stil und Gelassenheit.

Le Sereno est comme St Barth – le contraste intemporel et magique de la simplicité et du luxe, avec une combinaison rare de style et de décontraction.

Le Sereno es como St. Barthélemy –un contraste mágico e intemporal de simplicidad y lujo con una combinación exclusiva de estilo y sosiego.

Le Sereno, come St. Barth, è un contrasto magico e senza tempo di semplicità e lusso, una rara combinazione di stile e di relax.

Luxurious, spacious suites feature a generously sized living area with a sofa bed, a large wooden coffee table, a four poster bed, and a wooden deck.

Die luxuriösen Suiten haben einen großzügig geschnittenen Aufenthaltsbereich mit gemütlichem Sofa, großem hölzernen Couchtisch, Himmelbett und holzgedeckter Terrasse.

Les luxueuses suites disposent d'une salle de séjour spacieuse avec un confortable canapé, une grande table basse en bois, un lit à baldaquin et une terrasse en bois.

Las lujosas suites cuentan con una amplia estancia con un cómodo sofá, una gran mesita de centro de madera, cama con dosel y una terraza cubierta de madera

Le lussuose suite dispongono di uno spazioso soggiorno con un comodo divano, un grande tavolo di legno, letto a baldacchino e terrazza rivestita in legno.

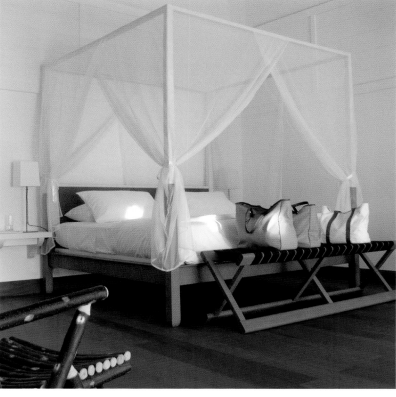

La Samanna

St. Martin, French West Indies

Ideally situated on a dazzling stretch of 55 beachfront acres and nestled among lush tropical gardens, this world-class resort is built on a steep cliff side that offers spectacular ocean views. This Mediterranean-style hotel has Spanish archways, mosaic and terra-cotta tiled floors. The 81 rooms, suites and villas are furnished with mahogany wood, teak imports and Caribbean wicker, and bathrooms with hand-painted Mexican tiles.

Die Lage dieses Anwesens ist einzigartig: Es befindet sich versteckt in einem üppigen, 22 Hektar großen, tropischen Garten, direkt am Meer. Da es auf einem Felsen thront, bietet das Resort eine spektakuläre Aussicht auf den Ozean. Die Gebäude sind im mediterranen Stil gehalten. Sie haben spanische Torbögen, Mosaike und mit Terrakotta geflieste Böden. Die 81 Suiten sind mit Mahagoni- und Teakmöbeln ausgestattet. Für besonderes Flair sorgen karibische Flechtmöbel sowie handbemalte mexikanische Fliesen im Badezimmer.

Ce domaine bénéficie d'un site exceptionnel : il se niche dans un grand jardin tropical luxuriant de 22 hectares, en bord de la mer. Comme il trône sur un rocher, le resort offre une vue spectaculaire sur l'océan. Les bâtiments affichent un style méditerranéen qu'illustrent des arcs de portail espagnols, des mosaïques et des sols pavés de terre cuite. Les meubles des 81 chambres, suites et villas sont en teck et en acajou. Des meubles tressés ainsi que des carreaux mexicains peints à la main dans les salles de bain leur confèrent un charme particulier.

La ubicación de esta mansión es única, oculta en un exuberante jardín tropical de 22 hectáreas, directamente junto al mar. Coronando una roca, el resort deja al descubierto unas vistas fantásticas del océano. Los edificios de estilo mediterráneo están dibujados con arcos de portal españoles, mosaicos y suelos embaldosados en terracota. Las 81 habitaciones, suites y villas están decoradas con muebles de caoba y teca. Los muebles tejidos de estilo caribeño y las baldosas mejicanas pintadas a mano de los cuartos de baño confieren al lugar un encanto especial.

La posizione di questo hotel è unica: si trova nascosto in un lussureggiante giardino tropicale di 22 ettari, direttamente sul mare. Arroccato su una rupe offre una spettacolare vista sull'oceano. Gli edifici sono realizzati in stile mediterraneo, con archi di gusto spagnoleggiante, mosaici e pavimenti di cotto. Le 81 camere, suite e ville sono arredate con mobili di mogano e teak. Mobili di vimini di ispirazione caraibica e, in bagno, piastrelle messicane dipinte a mano conferiscono un fascino particolare.

The white-washed stucco main building sits perched above a crescent-shaped beach, considered among the finest and most secluded in the world.

Das weiß getünchte, stuckverzierte Hauptgebäude schwebt über einem halbmondförmigen Strand. Das Hotel hat den Ruf, eines der besten und privatesten weltweit zu sein.

Le bâtiment principal, badigeonné de blanc et orné de stuc, surplombe une plage en forme de croissant de lune. L'hôtel a la réputation d'être l'un des meilleurs et des plus reculés au monde.

El edificio principal, blanqueado y adornado con estuco, parece pender sobre una playa en medialuna. El hotel tiene la reputación de ser uno de los mejores y más privados del mundo.

L'edificio principale, bianco e decorato con stucchi, è adagiato su una spiaggia a forma di mezzaluna. L'hotel è considerato uno dei migliori e più discreti del mondo.

Guests enjoy excellent French cuisine on a candlelit terrace overlooking Baie Longue (Long Bay). After dinner, the authentic Moroccan bar becomes a disco.

Die Gäste genießen die exzellente französische Küche auf einer von Kerzen beleuchteten Terrasse mit Blick auf die Baie Longue. Nach dem Abendessen wird die authentische marokkanische Bar zur Disko.

Les hôtes dégustent l'excellente cuisine française sur une terrasse éclairée aux bougies avec vue sur la Baie Longue. Après le dîner, l'authentique bar marocain se transforme en discothèque.

Los huéspedes disfrutan de la excelente cocina francesa en una terraza alumbrada con velas con vistas a la Baie Longue. Después de la cena, el auténtico bar marroquí se transforma en discoteca.

Gli ospiti gustano l'eccellente cucina francese a lume di candela su una terrazza con vista sulla Baie Longue. Dopo cena, il bar marocchino si trasforma in discoteca.

Anse Chastanet

St. Lucia, British West Indies

Enter any of the 49 rooms in this hillside hotel and your gaze is inevitably drawn to the pitons, the twin volcanic cones that shoot up from the sea to a height of about 2,300 feet. Only then can you appreciate the extraordinary feature of this Caribbean resort—trees grow unchecked though the rooms, glass-free windows blur distinctions between inside and out, and there are no televisions or radios. Numerous artists, including German painter Stefan Szczesny, have found inspiration amid these surroundings.

Wenn man eines der 49 Zimmer des an den Hang gebauten Hotels betritt, fällt der Blick zuerst auf die atemberaubenden Pitons, die zwei 700 Meter steil aus dem Meer herausragenden Felskegel. Dann erst erschließt sich das Außergewöhnliche dieses karibischen Resorts: Bäume dürfen durch die Räume wachsen, Fenster ohne Glas lassen die Übergänge von Innen- und Außenraum verschwimmen. Es gibt keinen Fernseher, kein Radio. Zahlreiche renommierte Künstler, unter ihnen der deutsche Maler Stefan Szczesny, ließen sich von diesem Ambiente inspirieren.

Lorsque le visiteur entre dans l'une des 49 chambres de l'hôtel construites sur le versant, son regard se pose en premier lieu sur les fabuleux pitons, quilles rocheuses raides de 700 mètres qui sortent de la mer. C'est seulement après que le visiteur découvre la particularité de ce complexe caribéen : les arbres peuvent pousser dans les pièces, les fenêtres ne possèdent pas de vitrage pour estomper les transitions de l'intérieur vers l'extérieur. Il n'y a pas de téléviseur, ni de radio. De nombreux artistes renommés, dont le peintre allemand Stefan Szczesny, ont puisé leur inspiration dans cette ambiance.

Al entrar en una de las 49 habitaciones del hotel situado en la ladera, la mirada se dirige en primer lugar a las Pitons, dos peñones que se elevan a 700 metros sobre el mar. Es entonces cuando se descubre lo extraordinario de estos resorts caribeños: árboles que crecen por los interiores y ventanas sin cristal que hacen que el interior y el exterior se confundan. Ausencia de televisión y radio. Numerosos artistas de renombre, entre ellos el pintor alemán Stefan Szczesny, se han dejado inspirar por este ambiente.

Entrando in una delle 49 stanze di questo hotel costruito in pendenza è impossibile non venire rapiti dalla vista sui due Piton, i coni vulcanici mozzafiato alti 700 metri che si ergono direttamente dalle acque. Solo dopo essersi ripresi si potrà scoprire ciò che rende insolito questo resort caraibico, nel quale gli alberi crescono attraverso fessure apposite nel tetto e finestre prive di vetri rendono fluidi i contorni del paesaggio mescolandolo agli interni. Non esistono radio o televisore. Numerosi gli artisti rinomati, fra cui il pittore tedesco Stefan Szczesny, che hanno tratto ispirazione dall'atmosfera che qui regna sovrana.

Views are dominated by dense rainforest and the pitons, St. Lucia's two signature landmarks. Twelve other lodges with walk-around verandas are built directly on the beach.

Über wuchernde Regenwälder schweift der Blick zum Wahrzeichen St. Lucias, den beiden Pitons. Zwölf weitere Bungalows mit umlaufenden Veranden wurden direkt an den Strand gebaut.

Le regard balaie la forêt vierge proliférante pour se poser sur l'emblème de St. Lucie, les deux pitons. 12 autres bungalows encadrés de vérandas ont été construits directement sur la plage.

Por encima de la espesa selva la vista se desplaza hacia el símbolo de Santa Lucía, las dos montañas Pitons. Los doce generosos bungalows con amplios balcones están ubicados justo al pie de playa.

Spaziando sulle lussureggianti foreste pluviali lo sguardo arriva fino ai vero simboli di Santa Lucia, i due Piton. Altri dodici bungalow con veranda circolare sono stati costruiti direttamente sulla spiaggia.

Set on a steep slope, these airy rooms offer guests a treehouse-like experience. All furnishings are made from teak, mahogany and cedar wood by local craftsmen.

Wie in einem Baumhaus können sich die Gäste der Zimmer fühlen, die in luftige Höhen an den Steilhang gebaut wurden. Sämtliche Möbel aus Teak-, Mahagoni- und Zedernholz wurden von einheimischen Handwerkern gefertigt.

Les visiteurs des chambres qui ont été construites sur le versant à des hauteurs aériennes ont l'impression d'habiter une cabane dans les arbres. Tous les meubles en teck, en acajou et en cèdre ont été réalisés par des artisans de la région.

Como en una casa ubicada en un árbol, así se podrán sentir los huéspedes en las habitaciones construidas en lo alto de la ladera escarpada. El mobiliario en madera de teca, caoba y cedro ha sido elaborado por artesanos nativos.

Come su una capanna sulla cima di un albero, è questa la sensazione provata dagli ospiti delle stanze costruite in posizione sopraelevata lungo il pendio scosceso. Tutti i mobili, costruiti in teak, mogano e cedro, sono opera di artigiani locali.

Camino Real México

Mexico City, Mexico

Mexico's Institute of Fine Arts recognizes this urban resort as one of the city's most important examples of contemporary architecture. The original building by Ricardo Legorreta had a distinctly museum-like feel, though a great deal of creative freedom was afforded to a new design in 2000. With square natural stone structures, wide staircases, colorful walls and huge paintings, not to mention blurred transitions between interiors and the park-like grounds, it is reminiscent of an Aztec temple.

Mexikos Institut für bildende Künste ordnet das urbane Resort als eines der wichtigsten zeitgenössischen Architekturbeispiele der Stadt ein. Schon der originale Entwurf von Ricardo Legorreta glich einem Museum. Die Bauherren ließen aber auch seiner Neugestaltung im Jahr 2000 viel Freiraum. Kubische Natursteinmauern, breite Treppen, farbige Betonwände und riesige Wandgemälde sowie weiche Übergänge zwischen dem Inneren und den parkartigen Freiräumen lassen Assoziationen zu Azteken-Tempeln aufkommen.

L'Institut des Beaux-Arts de Mexico considère ce complexe urbain comme l'un des exemples architecturaux contemporains les plus importants de la ville. La création originale de Ricardo Legorreta ressemblait déjà à un musée. Mais les maîtres d'ouvrage ont également pris beaucoup de liberté lors de sa rénovation en 2000. Des murs cubiques en pierre naturelle, de larges escaliers, des murs en béton coloré et de gigantesques peintures murales ainsi que de douces transitions entre l'intérieur et les espaces extérieurs, semblables à un parc, nous rappellent les temples aztèques.

El Instituto mejicano de artes plásticas ha calificado este resort urbano como uno de los más importantes referentes arquitectónicos contemporáneos de la ciudad. Ya el boceto original de Ricardo Legorreta parecía un museo. Los contratistas de la obra dejaron a la vez mucha libertad para su reforma en el año 2000. Los muros cúbicos de piedra natural, amplias escaleras, paredes de hormigón coloreado, extensos murales, así como el paso entre el interior y la zona exterior ajardinada recuerdan a templos aztecas.

L'Istituto di Belle Arti di Messico annovera questo resort situato nel centro di Città del Messico fra gli esempi più significativi di architettura contemporanea della città. Fin dal progetto originale, disegnato da Ricardo Legorreta, il complesso turistico di lusso sembrava assomigliare ad un museo. E quest'effetto non è stato che valorizzato dalla ristrutturazione del 2000, per la quale i committenti hanno concesso grande libertà d'azione. Strutture cubiche in pietra naturale, ampie scalinate, pareti in cemento colorato, enormi pitture a tutta parete nonché linee di passaggio fluide fra interni e giardini e spazi all'aperto fanno sorgere spontanee le associazioni con i templi aztechi.

An exclusive hotel complex is hidden behind these colorful walls, with 712 rooms and suites, 7 restaurants and bars, a park and a conference center with room for up to 1,500 people.

Hinter den farbigen Betonflächen verbirgt sich eine eigene Hotelwelt mit Park, Konferenzzentrum für bis zu 1500 Besucher, 712 Zimmern und Suiten, 7 Restaurants und Bars.

Derrière les surfaces en béton coloré se cache un complexe hôtelier avec un parc, un centre de conférences pouvant accueillir jusqu'à 1500 visiteurs, 712 chambres et suites, 7 restaurants et bars.

Detrás de esa superficie de hormigón de colores se esconde todo un complejo hotelero, con parque, centro de conferencias con capacidad para hasta 1500 asistentes, 712 habitaciones y suites, 7 restaurantes y bares.

Dietro le superfici di cemento colorato si cela un mondo tutto a sé completo di parco, centro conferenze con capienza fino a 1500 persone, 712 stanze e suite, 7 ristoranti e bar.

Thanks to the pebbled waters visible through its glass floor, the Blue Bar is an architectural attraction itself. The atmospheric Moonbar on the hotel roof is ideal for mixing and mingling in the evening.

Die Blue Bar ist schon architektonisch ein Anziehungspunkt durch ihren Glasboden über einer Wasserfläche mit Kieselsteingrund. Abendlicher Treffpunkt ist die stimmungsvolle Moonbar auf dem Gebäudedach.

Du point de vue architectural, le Blue Bar constitue un pôle d'attraction avec son sol en verre placé au-dessus d'une étendue d'eau dont le fond est parsemé de galets. Installé sur le toit du bâtiment, le Moonbar romantique le lieu de rendez-vous du soir.

El Blue Bar, con su suelo de cristal sobre una superficie de agua con guijarros en el fondo, es toda una atracción arquitectónica. Por las noches el acogedor Moonbar en la azotea se convierte en el punto de encuentro.

Il Blue Bar è di grande attrattiva, anche solo dal punto di vista architettonico per i suoi pavimenti in vetro sopra una superficie acquea con fondo acciottolato. Di fascino tutto lunare nelle ore serali: il suggestivo Moonbar sul tetto della struttura.

Sheraton Centro Histórico

Mexico City, Mexico

This hotel overlooking Alameda Park has 457 rooms, most of which offer great views of the city's downtown district with its 182 meter skyscraper Torre Latinoamericana and picturesque opera house. This makes it the ideal base for guests looking to explore Mexico City's historic center. Although built as a conference hotel with accommodation for up to 2,000 people, its contemporary architecture, color scheme and design concept evoke a luxurious relaxed club atmosphere.

Wer das historische Zentrum der Stadt erkunden möchte, dem gewähren bereits die meisten der 457 Zimmer Aussicht auf den Alameda Park und „Downtown" mit seinem 182 Meter hohen Torre Latinoamericana und dem pittoresken Opernhaus. Obwohl als Veranstaltungshotel mit Räumen für bis zu 2000 Personen angelegt, erzeugt die zeitgenössische Architektur mit ihrem Farb- und Materialkonzept eine entspannte Clubatmosphäre.

Ceux qui souhaitent explorer le centre historique de la ville profiteront déjà dans la plupart des 457 chambres d'une vue sur le parc Alameda et le centre-ville avec la Torre Latinoamericana de 182 mètres de hauteur et l'opéra pittoresque. Hôtel conçu à l'origine pour l'organisation de manifestations avec des pièces pouvant accueillir jusqu'à 2000 personnes, l'architecture contemporaine crée une atmosphère de club décontractée avec son concept de couleurs et de matériaux.

Para aquellos que deseen explorar el centro histórico de la ciudad, la mayoría de las 457 habitaciones ya le ofrecen una vista panorámica del parque Alameda y el "downtown" con su Torre Latinoamericana de 182 metros de altura y su pintoresca ópera. Si bien el hotel con capacidad para hasta 2000 personas fue diseñado para celebrar eventos, su estilo arquitectónico a base de colores y materiales contemporáneos crea la atmósfera relajante de un club.

Chi vuole esplorare il centro storico non avrà che da cominciare affacciandosi alla finestra di quasi tutte le 457 stanze con vista sul parco di Alameda e su "downtown", con la Torre Latinoamericana alta 182 metri e il pittoresco teatro d'opera. Sebbene per impostazione un hotel congressuale dotato di sale con capienza fino a 2000 persone, la cifra architettonica ispirata al design contemporaneo, sottolineata dalla scelta cromatica e dei materiali, è determinante per la disinvolta atmosfera club magistralmente ricreata.

Two floors of restaurants, cafes, shops and bars as well as the conference rooms are centered around the main atrium lobby.

Mit der Atrium-Lobby als Mittelpunkt erstrecken sich auf zwei Etagen Restaurants, Cafeteria, Shops und Bars sowie die Veranstaltungsräume.

Les restaurants, la cafétéria, les magasins et les bars, ainsi que les salles prévues pour les manifestations, ont été aménagées sur deux étages, au centre un lobby atrium.

Desde el vestíbulo atrio como centro se distribuyen entre dos plantas los restaurantes, cafeterías, tiendas y bares, además de varios salones de celebraciones.

Attorno al fulcro costituito dalla lobby a forma di atrio si distribuiscono su due piani diversi ristoranti, una caffetteria, negozi, bar nonché sale conferenza.

Mexico City as far as the eye can see. The views from the rooms on the upper levels of this 24-storey skyscraper give you some idea of just how vast this bustling metropolis really is.

Mexico City so weit das Auge reicht. Beim Blick aus den Zimmern der höheren Etagen des 24-stöckigen Hochhauses bekommt man ein Gefühl für die Größe der Millionenmetropole.

Mexico City, à perte de vue. Le panorama offert par les chambres des étages supérieurs de l'immeuble de 24 étages donne une impression des dimensions de la mégapole.

México City en todo su esplendor. Desde las habitaciones de los pisos más altos del rascacielos de 24 plantas se puede apreciar la magnitud de esta gran metrópoli.

Città del Messico a perdita d'occhio. La vista panoramica sulla città dalle stanze ai piani superiori del grattacielo alto 24 piani dà la sensazione della reale estensione di questa megalopoli.

Hotelito Desconocido

Puerto Vallarta, Mexico

The fan above the mosquito net is the only thing that runs on electricity here. Keys are as unnecessary as laptops and room service is simplicity itself: simply hoist a little red flag and wait for your coffee to arrive. This interpretation of an idyllic fishing village by Italian fashion designer Marcello Murzilli offers its mostly spoiled clientele the chance to rediscover the charm of simplicity. Guests revel in the stripped-down luxury afforded by the marshland and miles of sandy beaches.

Einzig der Ventilator über dem Moskitonetz wird hier von Strom angetrieben. In solcher Umgebung sind Schlüssel genauso überflüssig wie Laptops und der Zimmer-service funktioniert bestechend einfach: Rotes Fähnchen hochziehen und der Kaffee kommt. In dieser Inkarnation eines fantastischen Fischerdorfs des italienischen Mo-dedesigners Marcello Murzilli entdecken die meist reichlich verwöhnten Gäste den Reiz der Einfachheit wieder; zwischen Sümpfen und kilometerlangen Sandstränden zelebrieren sie ihren „Barfuß-Luxus".

Ici, seul le ventilateur placé au-dessus de la moustiquaire fonctionne à l'électricité. Dans un environnement de ce type, les clés sont tout autant superflues que les ordina-teurs portables, et le service de chambre fonctionne de manière extrêmement simple : il suffit de hisser le petit drapeau rouge et le café arrive. Dans cette incarnation d'un fantastique village de poissonniers du styliste de mode italien Marcello Murzilli, les visiteurs, souvent très riches, redécouvrent le charme de la simplicité ; ils profitent de leur « luxe à pieds nus » entre les marécages et les plages de sable long de plusieurs kilomètres.

Sólo el ventilador sobre la mosquitera se acciona eléctricamente. Aquí las llaves son tan innecesarias como los portátiles. El servicio de habitaciones funciona de forma sen-cilla: se levanta la banderita roja y llega el café. En esta recreación de un maravilloso pueblo de pescadores del diseñador de moda italiano Marcello Murzilli, los mimados huéspedes redescubren el atractivo de la sencillez; entre pantanos y kilométricas playas de arena experimentan el lujo de caminar descalzos.

Solo il ventilatore a soffitto sopra la zanzariera è alimentato a energia elettrica. In un ambiente in cui le chiavi sono tanto superflue quanto i laptop, il servizio in camera è di una semplicità affascinante: sollevando una bandierina rossa si sarà subito accontentati con una bella tazza di caffè. In un contesto che vuole essere l'incarnazione di un fantastico villaggio di pescatori ad opera dello stilista italiano Marcello Murzilli, gli ospiti solitamente straviziati riscoprono il fascino della semplicità: come celebrando un rituale alla ricerca del "lusso a piedi scalzi" fra terreni acquitrinosi e spiagge chilometriche.

The 100-acre grounds are reserved exclusively for guests and resort em-ployees. Limiting the development to just 24 stilted dwellings ensures an intimate atmosphere.

Auf dem 40 Hektar großen Grundstück bleiben die Gäste und Resortan-gestellten unter sich. Die Beschränkung auf nur 24 Pfahlbauten bewahrt eine intime Atmosphäre.

Sur ce terrain de 40 hectares, les visiteurs et les employés du complexe restent entre eux. Le fait d'avoir limité les constructions sur pilotis au nombre de 24 permet de créer une atmosphère intime.

En las 40 hectáreas de extensión, huéspedes y empleados disfrutan del aislamiento. El ambiente de intimidad queda preservado gracias a la restricción a sólo 24 construcciones de pilotes.

Su un'estensione di 40 ettari, ospiti e dipendenti del resort vivono a stretto contatto. Il limite fissato a sole 24 palafitte consente di preservare un'atmosfera di intimità.

After dinner, returning to the beach lodges is a breeze—simply call the boat butler and let him row you back over the lagoon.

Wer nach dem Dinner zurück in sein Stranddomizil möchte, kann sich vom Boat-Butler über die Lagune rudern lassen.

Les personnes souhaitant rentrer après le dîner à leur domicile sur la plage peuvent se faire raccompagner par un « serviteur en bateau » traversera la lagune à la rame.

Quien desee volver a su estancia en la playa después de cenar podrá pedirle a un asistente que lo desplace en barca de remos por la laguna.

Chi dopo una lauta cenetta desidera tornare nella sua dimora sulla spiaggia può farsi accompagnare oltre la laguna a colpi di remo dal "boat butler".

Esencia

Riviera Maya, Mexico

Formerly the Caribbean residence of an Italian duchess, Esencia was transformed into a boutique retreat by Samir Saab's ProHotel Group. Great care was taken to retain the charm, with only two holiday villas and 20 suites added to the main house, which itself is home to nine suites. The extra suites in this 50-acre resort complex are grouped in pairs in mediterranean-style buildings. With dazzling white interiors and exteriors, they all boast a private plunge pool while many enjoy sea views.

Früher war es das Karibikdomizil einer italienischen Herzogin. Die Betreiber von ProHotel um Samir Saab haben bei ihrer Umnutzung darauf geachtet, dieses Flair zu erhalten und dem Haupthaus mit seinen neun Suiten auf dem 20 Hektar großen Grundstück nur zwei Ferienvillen und 20 weitere Suiten hinzugefügt, die jeweils paarweise in Gebäuden im mediterranen Stil untergebracht sind. Die Innenräume erstrahlen genauso in Weiß wie die Fassade, alle haben ihren eigenen Erfrischungspool, viele von ihnen sogar mit Meerblick.

C'était autrefois le domicile caribéen d'une duchesse italienne. Avec Samir Saab, les exploitants du ProHotel ont veillé lors de la rénovation à conserver ce charme et n'ont ajouté au bâtiment principal, qui compte neuf suites sur un terrain de 20 hectares, que deux villas de vacances et 20 autres suites qui sont regroupées par deux dans des bâtiments de style méditerranéen. Comme la façade, les pièces intérieures sont resplendissantes de blanc immaculé, toutes les suites ont leur propre piscine rafraîchissante et la plupart d'entre elles ont même vue sur la mer.

En otros tiempos, esta era la residencia caribeña de una duquesa italiana. Durante su remodelación, los operadores de ProHotel, con su presidente Samir Saab, han procurado conservar ese encanto. Al edificio principal con nueve suites, construido sobre una amplia superficie de 20 hectáreas, se le han añadido únicamente dos villas vacacionales y 20 amplias suites, dispuestas de dos en dos en edificios de estilo mediterráneo. Tanto los espacios interiores como las fachadas lucen blanco resplandeciente. Además, todas las suites disponen de su propia piscina, muchas de ellas incluso con vistas al mar.

Originariamente si trattava della dimora caribica di una duchessa italiana. Un particolare cui lo staff di supporto del presidente Samir Saab della catena ProHotel ha prestato molta cura durante la ristrutturazione, con l'intento di preservarne il fascino. Così, al complesso principale costituito da nove suite su un terreno di 20 ettari si sono aggiunte solo due ville e altre 20 suite, suddivise in edifici da due in stile mediterraneo: gli interni quanto le facciate di un bianco accecante, dotate di piscina privata per rinfrescarsi e molte addirittura con vista sul mare.

The poolside restaurant and the powdery sand beaches typical of Riviera Maya are just a stone's throw from the main house.

Vom Hauptgebäude sind es nur wenige Schritte zum Poolrestaurant und zu dem für die Riviera Maya typischen Pudersandstrand.

Seuls quelques pas séparent le bâtiment principal du restaurant de la piscine et de la plage typique de sable fin de la Rivière Maya.

A tan sólo unos pasos del edificio central se encuentra el restaurante de la piscina y la playa de fina arena típica de la Riviera Maya.

Dall'edificio principale bastano pochi passi per arrivare al ristorante al bordo piscina o alla spiaggia fine polverosa tipica della Riviera Maya.

All 29 suites boast a small terrace with a sofa, while suites in the main house have brick-vaulted ceilings. Even the lounge in the main building with its small library is decked out in white.

Die Suiten im Hauptgebäude sind mit Ziegelsteinen überwölbt, alle 29 haben eine kleine Terrasse mit Sofa. Auch die Lounge mit ihrer kleinen Bibliothek im Hauptgebäude ist ganz in Weiß gehalten.

Les 29 suites du bâtiment principal sont recouvertes de tuiles et possèdent chacune une petite terrasse avec divan. Même le lounge avec sa petite bibliothèque dans le bâtiment principal est entièrement blanc.

Las suites del edificio central están abovedadas en ladrillo y cuentan todas las 29 con una pequeña terraza con sofá. También la sala con su pequeña biblioteca albergada en el edificio principal está decorada en blanco en su totalidad.

Le suite dell'edificio principale, con soffitto a volta con mattoni a vista, hanno tutte e nove una piccola terrazza con divano. Anche la lounge con piccola biblioteca dell'edificio principale è rigorosamente in bianco.

Ikal del Mar

Riviera Maya, Mexico

This tranquil jungle refuge is set just a few miles north of the party town of Playa del Carmen. Ikal del Mar, which means poetry of the sea, is so out-of-the-way that only local drivers know how to get there. Lined with ferns and cacti, paths lead from reception to the spa, pool, beach restaurant and the 30 bohíos. These luxury huts, dedicated to poets such as Neruda, Dario and Alberti, are a fusion of Mayan and modern architecture. All have a private plunge pool and open-air shower.

Nur wenige Kilometer nördlich der Partyhochburg Playa del Carmen herrscht erholsame Ruhe im Dschungel. Ikal del Mar – zu Deutsch „Gedichte des Meeres" – liegt so versteckt, dass man es nur mit ortskundigem Chauffeur findet. Zwischen Farnen und Kakteen führen Pfade vom Empfang zum Spa, Pool, Strandrestaurant und den 30 Bohios. Diese, Dichtern wie Neruda, Dario und Alberti gewidmeten, Luxus-Hütten sind eine Kombination aus Mayakonstruktion und moderner Architektur. Alle haben ihren eigenen Erfrischungspool und eine Freiluftdusche.

À quelques kilomètres seulement au nord du bastion de la fête Playa del Carmen règne le calme reposant de la jungle. Ikal del Mar (en français : « les poèmes de la mer ») est si bien caché qu'on ne le trouve que si l'on est accompagné d'un chauffeur connaissant les lieux. Au milieu des fougères et des cactus, des sentiers mènent les visiteurs de la réception au spa, à la piscine, au restaurant de la plage et aux 30 bohios. Ces cabanes de luxe, dédiées à des poètes tels que Neruda, Dario et Alberti, associent la construction Maya à l'architecture moderne. Tous possèdent leur propre piscine rafraîchissante et une douche en plein air.

A tan sólo unos kilómetros al norte de la bulliciosa Playa del Carmen, impera la tranquilidad relajante en la jungla. Ikal del Mar, en español, "poemas del mar" – yace tan escondido que sólo se puede encontrar con un guía local. Un camino de helechos y cactus conducen desde la recepción hacia el spa, la piscina, el restaurante de la playa y los 30 bohíos. Estas cabañas de lujo dedicadas a escritores como Neruda, Darío y Alberti, constituyen una armoniosa combinación entre el estilo de construcción maya y la arquitectura moderna. Todas cuentan con piscina propia y ducha al aire libre.

Solo pochi chilometri a nord dalla festaiola Playa del Carmen regna la calma assoluta della giungla: Ikal del Mar, che tradotto letteralmente significa "poesie del mare", è così ben nascosta che è possibile trovarla solo se guidati da uno chauffeur pratico del luogo. Fra felci e cactus, si dipanano sentieri che portano dalla reception alla Spa, alla piscina, al ristorante sulla spiaggia e ai 29 bohio. Queste capanne di lusso, dedicate a poeti come Neruda, Dario e Alberti, sono una combinazione fra le costruzioni maya e l'architettura moderna; esse sono inoltre tutte dotate di piscina privata e doccia all'aperto.

Sunbathers have *a choice between the pool overlooking the sea or straw-roofed loungers on the white sandy beach.*

Zum Sonnenbaden *hat man die Wahl zwischen dem Pool mit Meerblick oder einem Liegebett mit Strohdach am weißen Sandstrand.*

Pour prendre *un bain de soleil, on peut choisir entre la piscine avec vue sur la mer ou une chaise longue avec toit de paille sur la plage de sable blanc.*

Para tomar *el sol se puede optar por la piscina con vistas al mar o las hamacas con sombrilla de paja en la playa de arena blanca.*

Per i *bagni di sole, l'alternativa è fra la piscina con vista mare e i lettini con tetto di paglia posizionati sulla spiaggia di sabbia candida.*

Diners are treated to highly-praised cuisine, and can also enjoy their meals accompanied by a moonlit view of the sea. Cozumel Island is visible in the distance.

Wer hier speist, kommt nicht nur in den Genuss einer viel gelobten Küche, sondern kann mit seinem Blick auch dem Mondschein über das Meer folgen. Im Hintergrund ist die Insel Cozumel zu sehen.

Les personnes qui déjeunent ici dégustent non seulement une cuisine très appréciée, mais elles peuvent également regarder le clair de lune se refléter dans la mer. L'île de Cozumel est visible à l'horizon.

Quienes comen aquí, no viene tan sólo por el placer de disfrutar de una cocina de renombre, sino para contemplar además el reflejo de la luna sobre el mar, con la isla Cozumel como telón de fondo.

Pasteggiare in questo luogo non significa solo gustare una cucina tanto elogiata, ma piuttosto seguire con lo sguardo la scia del chiaro di luna riflessa sul mare. Sullo sfondo è possibile scorgere l'isola di Cozumel.

The restrained color scheme has an elegant and calming effect. Thanks to the cone-shaped roofs, a refreshing draft of air circulates in the bohíos and the Maya spa.

Die zurückhaltende Farbgestaltung wirkt edel und ruhig. Dank der Spitzdächer herrscht in den Bohios und im Maya Spa eine erfrischende Luftzirkulation.

L'utilisation discrète des couleurs procure une impression d'élégance et de calme. Les toits pointus garantissent une circulation rafraîchissante de l'air dans les bohios et le spa Maya.

La discreta composición de colores proporciona distinción y sosiego. Los puntiagudos techos de los bohíos y del spa maya proporcionan la circulación de aire fresco.

Le cromie tutte modulate sui toni smorzati conferiscono eleganza e sobrietà. I tetti a punta dei bohio e del centro benessere Maya favoriscono la circolazione dell'aria, creando un piacevole effetto rinfrescante.

Hacienda Temozón

Yucatán, Mexico

This former 17th century cattle ranch has been transformed into a luxury resort, leaving little trace of its original agricultural use. Famous figures from all over the world come to the Hacienda in search of refuge and tranquility amid natural surroundings. A total of 26 suites, some of which have a private pool and small garden, are located in the main ranch building and the surrounding houses. This retreat is an ideal base for walks to the Mayan ruins or for exploring the barren scenery by bike.

Die ehemalige Rinderfarm aus dem 17. Jahrhundert erinnert nach dem Um- und Ausbau kaum noch an den ursprünglichen landwirtschaftlichen Zweck. Das Haupt- und die Nebengebäude der Hazienda beherbergen mittlerweile Prominenz aus aller Welt, die die Abgeschiedenheit und Ruhe in der Natur und in einer der insgesamt 26 Suiten des Anwesens suchen. Einige der Suiten haben einen eigenen Pool und einen kleinen Garten. Ganz in der Nähe kann man auf den Spuren der Mayas wandern oder die karge Landschaft mit dem Rad erkunden.

L'ancienne ferme de bœufs du 17ème siècle rappelle encore l'objectif agricole d'origine, même après la rénovation et l'agrandissement. Le bâtiment principal et les bâtiments annexes de la hacienda hébergent désormais les personnes célèbres du monde entier qui recherchent l'isolement et le calme dans la nature et dans l'une des 26 suites du domaine. Quelques suites ont leur propre piscine et un petit jardin. À proximité de la ferme, on peut effectuer des randonnées à la recherche de traces des Mayas ou explorer le paysage aride à vélo.

La antigua granja de ganado vacuno que data del siglo XVII, apenas nos recuerda, tras de su reforma y ampliación, la actividad para la que originalmente estaba destinada. El edificio principal de la hacienda y el contiguo a la misma, acogen a personalidades de todo el mundo que buscan la soledad y tranquilidad en la naturaleza y en una de las 26 suites. Algunas de ellas tienen su propia piscina y un pequeño jardín. En los alrededores se pueden realizar excursiones siguiendo las huellas de la civilización maya, o bien descubrir el árido paisaje en bicicleta.

Dopo l'ampliamento e la ristrutturazione dell'ex allevamento di manzi del XVII secolo non rimangono praticamente tracce che ne ricordino l'uso agricolo. L'edificio principale e la dépendance dell'hacienda ospitano frattanto vip provenienti da tutto il mondo alla ricerca della calma e della tranquillità che sperano di trovare qui, nella natura e in una delle 28 suite della tenuta. Alcune delle suite dispongono di una piscina privata e di un piccolo giardino. Nelle dirette vicinanze è possibile avventurarsi sulle tracce dei Maya o esplorare il paesaggio brullo in bicicletta.

The original main building of the ranch is once again the heart of the Hacienda.

Das ehemalige Hauptgebäude der Farm ist auch heute wieder der Mittelpunkt der Hazienda.

Aujord'hui, l'ancien bâtiment principal de la ferme est redevenu le point central de la hacienda.

El antiguo edificio principal de la granja es también hoy el punto central de la hacienda.

L'edificio principale dell'ex azienda agricola costituisce ancora oggi il fulcro dell'Hacienda.

The interior *is characterized by Mexican symbolism and matching decor.*

Zurückhaltend *wurde mit mexikanischer Symbolik und entsprechendem Dekor im Innenraum umgegangen.*

La symbolique *mexicaine et le décor intérieur correspondant sont discrets.*

En el *interior existe una decoración discreta inspirada en el simbolismo mejicano.*

Estremamente sobrio *il ricorso alla simbologia messicana e l'impiego dei simboli come motivi decorativi nell'arredamento degli interni.*

Turtle Inn

Placencia, Belize

Francis Ford Coppola sends his regards, along with a warm invitation to visit the luxury resort that he owns. Film directors of his ilk are globetrotters at heart, which is why he chose Bali as the inspiration for his Caribbean sanctuary. Beneath the deep and densely thatched roofs of each cabana lies a labyrinth of rooms, decorated with carvings and exotic crafted works in warm tones. The backdrop of pools and spa facilities is so luxurious, it could almost have been taken from an exotic film set.

Francis Ford Coppola lässt grüßen. Besser gesagt: Er lädt sogar ein in die Anlage, die er besitzt. Und da Regisseure wie er Globetrotter im Geiste sind, erschuf er aus der karibischen Destination ein balinesisch inspiriertes Refugium. Unter den dichten, tiefen Reetdächern wartet in jeder Hütte ein weitläufiges Geflecht von Räumen. Ihre Ausstattung spielt mit Schnitzarbeiten und tropischem Handwerk in warmen Tönen. Luxuriös sind auch die Bad- und Poolanlagen – und absolut kulissenträchtig.

Francis Ford Coppola vous salue. Ou plutôt : il vous invite dans le complexe dont il est le propriétaire. Étant donné que les metteurs en scène comme lui sont des globe-trotters dans l'âme, il a fait de la destination caribéenne un refuge d'inspiration balinaise. Dans chaque hutte, le visiteur découvre de nombreuses pièces imbriquées les unes dans les autres sous des toits en roseaux bas et épais. La décoration met en valeur les sculptures sur bois et l'artisanat tropical dans des tons chauds. Les salles de bain et les piscines sont tout aussi luxueuses et feraient de superbes coulisses.

Francis Ford Coppola es aquí anfitrión, mejor dicho, extiende invitaciones para visitar el lugar que le pertenece. Y puesto que directores como él son grandes trota-mundos de la imaginación, Coppola ha hecho de este destino caribeño un refugio de inspiración balinesa. Bajo los gruesos y compactos tejados de caña en cada cabaña se encuentra una amplia red de habitaciones. La decoración juega con trabajos en madera y piezas de artesanía tropical en tonos cálidos. Los cuartos de baño y las instalaciones de la piscina son igualmente lujosos y dignos escenarios de película.

Con tanti saluti da parte di Francis Ford Coppola. Anzi: su suo invito, visto che il resort è di sua proprietà. E poiché i registi come lui sono tutti globetrotter nello spi-rito, l'idea di costruirsi un rifugio ispirato allo stile balinese nella meta caraibica gli sembrò più che naturale. Sotto i bassi e fitti tetti di paglia di ogni capanna si districa un vasto intreccio di stanze. L'arredamento è tutto giocato sui motivi ad intaglio e su pezzi d'artigianato tropicale in calde tonalità. Di gran lusso i bagni e la piscina… assolutamente scenografici.

The exposed thatched roofs are a typically Belize element of the resort. Every cabana opens out onto a spacious veranda.

Die offenen Reetdächer kennzeichnen den Belizer Stil der Anlage. Jede Hütte besitzt eine großzügige Veranda.

Les toits en roseaux ouverts soulignent le style bélizien du complexe. Chaque cabane possède une véranda généreuse.

Los tejados de caña abiertos marcan el estilo de Belize de los edificios. Cada cabaña cuenta con un amplio balcón.

I tetti di paglia aperti sono caratteristici dello stile beliziano che con-traddistingue il resort. Ogni capanna dispone di una spaziosa veranda.

A hotel concept conceived by Francis Ford Coppola—comfortable furnishings, open rooms and idyllic natural surroundings.

So empfängt Francis Ford Coppola seine Gäste: bequem eingerichtet, mit offenen Räumen, von einem Naturidyll umrahmt.

Voici comment Francis Ford Coppola accueille ses visiteurs : confort de l'aménagement, avec des pièces ouvertes, au beau milieu d'un endroit idyllique et naturel.

Así recibe Francis Ford Coppola a sus invitados: estancias abiertas con todas las comodidades, en un marco natural idílico.

È così che Francis Ford Coppola riceve i suoi ospiti: arredamento confortevole, stanze aperte e l'idillio della natura a fare da cornice.

Emiliano

São Paulo, Brazil

This narrow, architecturally impressive building towers high in the São Paulo skyline. Located in the heart of the city's most fashionable district alongside designer-label boutiques and international banks, it has 38 spacious rooms and 19 even larger suites in the upper part of the building. Highlights include the classical modern restaurant that serves exquisite Italian cuisine and the striking hotel bar. A top-floor spa offers relaxing indulgences and stunning views of the city below.

Das schmale, architektonisch eindrucksvolle Gebäude ragt wie ein Fingerzeig auf. Es liegt mitten im besten Viertel von São Paulo, dort, wo sich die Designläden und Banken der Welt präsentieren. Im oberen Teil des Gebäudes wartet das Hotel mit 38 großen Zimmern und 19 noch größeren Suiten auf. Glanzstücke der Adresse sind das klassisch-moderne Restaurant mit feiner italienischer Küche sowie die Bar mit ungewöhnlichem Design. Als einzigartig erweist sich zudem der Ausblick beim Relaxen in dem Spa in der obersten Etage.

Le bâtiment étroit à l'architecture impressionnante se dresse comme s'il souhaitait indiquer son emplacement. Il se trouve au beau milieu du meilleur quartier de São Paulo, là où les magasins de design et les banques mondiales sont représentés. Dans la partie supérieure du bâtiment, l'hôtel comprend 38 grandes chambres et 19 suites encore plus grandes. Les chefs-d'œuvre de cette adresse sont le restaurant de style classique et moderne avec sa délicieuse cuisine italienne, ainsi que le bar affichant un design inhabituel. En outre, la vue que nous offre le spa du dernier étage est incomparable.

Este estrecho e impactante edificio se eleva como queriendo lanzar una advertencia. Está situado en el mejor barrio de São Paulo, allí donde las boutiques de los diseñadores y los bancos más importantes del mundo están presentes. En la parte superior del edificio se encuentra el hotel con 38 habitaciones grandes y 19 suites aún más amplias. Las piezas de mayor atractivo de este hotel son el restaurante típicamente moderno de alta cocina italiana y el bar, de extraordinario diseño. Las vistas desde el relajante spa de la planta superior constituyen una experiencia única.

L'edificio sottile, architettonicamente imponente, si erige in posizione strategica nel miglior quartiere di San Paolo, là dove negozi di design e banche internazionali si presentano nella loro veste migliore. Situato ai piani superiori, l'hotel dispone di 38 stanze spaziose e 19 suite di ancor più ampia metratura. Fiore all'occhiello dell'Emiliano sono il ristorante classico-moderno con raffinata cucina italiana e il bar dal design insolito. Notevole la vista panoramica sulla città di cui si può godere in pieno relax nella Spa all'ultimo piano.

Carefully appointed with defined furnishings, the spacious hotel lobby is a gem of contemporary design.

Die Lobby des Hotels ist geprägt von zeitgemäßem Design, weitläufig und pointiert in der Auswahl der Einrichtungsstücke.

Le lobby de l'hôtel présente un design contemporain, vaste et précis dans le choix des meubles.

Un diseño contemporáneo caracteriza al lobby, espacio extenso y refinado en la elección del mobiliario.

La lobby dell'hotel si contraddistingue per l'atmosfera in cui predomina il design contemporaneo, nella sua accezione più ampia ma allo stesso tempo dettagliata come dimostra la scelta dei complementi d'arredo.

From bedroom to bath the spacious 900-square-feet suites are presented in warm wooden tones and exclusive decor.

Die 84 Quadratmeter großen Suiten zeigen sich in warmen Holztönen und bieten ein exklusives Interieur, vom Schlafzimmer bis zum Bad.

Les suites de 84 mètres carrés présentent des tons de bois chauds et offrent un intérieur exclusif, de la chambre à coucher à la salle de bain.

Las amplias suites de 84 metros cuadrados lucen en tonos madera cálidos con un exclusivo interior tanto en los dormitorios como en los cuartos de baño.

Nelle suite ampie ben 84 metri quadrati predominano le tonalità calde del legno. Gli interni sono arredati all'insegna dell'esclusività: dalla camera da letto fino al bagno.

Fasano

São Paulo, Brazil

Although originally hailing from Italy, the Fasano family has dominated the gourmet scene in Brazil's largest city for over a century now. The Fasano hotel has a fine reputation to live up to and it does not disappoint: its Italian restaurant is said to be the finest in South America. Designed by two internationally acclaimed architects, Isay Weinfeld and Marcio Kogan, the hotel is a fusion of classic details with elegant contemporary stylings. Design highlights include the jazz bar and the spa.

Eigentlich stammt die Familie Fasano aus Italien. Doch seit über einem Jahrhundert dominiert sie bereits die gehobene Gastronomie in Brasiliens Metropole. Das Hotel steht folglich für höchste Ansprüche: So besitzt es gar den Ruf, das beste italienische Restaurant in Südamerika zu beherbergen. Mit Isay Weinfeld und Marcio Kogan gestalteten zudem zwei international renommierte Designer das Hotel, klassisch in den Details und zeitgenössisch-elegant im Stil. Ganz besondere gestalterische Highlights sind die Jazz-Bar und das Spa.

La famille Fasano est d'origine italienne. Mais depuis plus d'un siècle, elle domine la gastronomie de luxe de la métropole brésilienne. L'hôtel est par conséquent connu pour ses exigences extrêmement élevées : il a même la réputation d'héberger le meilleur restaurant italien d'Amérique du Sud. Ce sont en outre deux architectes d'intérieur renommés au niveau international, Isay Weinfeld et Marcio Kogan, qui ont aménagé l'hôtel, détails classiques et style à la fois contemporain et élégant. Le bar de jazz et le spa sont des créations particulièrement réussies.

En realidad, la familia Fasano procede de Italia. Pero desde hace más de un siglo son los máximos representantes de la alta cocina de la metrópoli brasileña. En consecuencia, el hotel responde a las demandas más exigentes, de ahí que disfrute de la reputación de albergar el mejor restaurante italiano de Sudamérica. Isay Weinfeld y Marcio Kogan, dos diseñadores internacionales de renombre, fueron los encargados de proyectar este hotel de detalles clásicos y un estilo elegante y contemporáneo. El jazz-bar y el spa destacan por su creativo diseño.

A dire il vero la famiglia Fasano è di origine italiana, sebbene domini ormai da oltre un secolo la scena culinaria della metropoli brasiliana essendosi affermata nel settore della ristorazione ad alto livello. Di conseguenza, anche l'hotel non poteva suscitare minori aspettative. Ben riposte, a giudicare dal fatto che il ristorante che esso ospita gode fama di essere il miglior ristorante italiano di tutto il Sudamerica. Inoltre, l'hotel deve il suo styling a due grandi nomi internazionali del design, Isay Weinfeld e Marcio Kogan, cui si deve l'atmosfera classica nel dettaglio e chic contemporanea nello stile. Veri highlight di creatività artistica: il jazz bar e la Spa.

The interior design concept by Isay Weinfeld is based on distance and defined decor.

Die Raumgestaltung von Isay Weinfeld steht für Weite und pointiertes Interieur.

L'agencement des pièces par Isay Weinfeld met l'accent sur la place disponible et la précision de l'intérieur.

La decoración de Isay Weinfeld persigue la amplitud y el realce del interior.

Gli interni realizzati da Isay Weinfeld si contraddistinguono per spaziosità e capacità di sintesi.

The spa features an exclusive designer seating concept by Heinz Wegner.

Das Spa bietet seltene Design-Sitzgelegenheiten von Heinz Wegner.

Le spa comprend quelques rares sièges design de Heinz Wegner.

El spa cuenta con insólitos asientos de diseño de Heinz Wegner.

La Spa sorprende con le sedute rare firmate Heinz Wegner.

Faena Hotel + Universe

Buenos Aires, Argentina

Even the entrance to this luxury hotel looks like a cathedral. Alan Faena, founder of the fashion label Via Vai, has transformed an old grain warehouse into Buenos Aires's only complete lifestyle hotel. Conceived by Philippe Stark, its design is tinged with belle époque accents, evident from the white-gold pomp of the bistro and the furnishings. A temple to pleasure in its purest form, the hotel has a stage, spa, boutique and poolside bar as well as opulent rooms for hosting events.

Bereits das Entree wirkt wie eine Kathedrale. Alan Faena, Gründer des Modelabels Via Vai, erschuf aus einem alten Getreidespeicher ein für Buenos Aires bisher einmaliges Lifestyle-Universum. In das Design von Philippe Starck mischt sich ein Hauch von Belle Époque, sichtbar am weiß-goldenen Pomp des Bistros und dem Mobiliar. Das Hotel stellt ein komplettes Areal für ein Leben der Extraklasse dar: mit Bühne, Spa, Boutique, Poolbar und edel anmutenden Räumen für Events.

L'entrée nous rappelle déjà une cathédrale. Alan Faena, créateur du label de mode Via Vai, a transformé un ancien grenier à céréales en un univers lifestyle jusqu'ici unique pour Buenos Aires. Des caractéristiques de la Belle Époque, reconnaissables à la pompe blanche et dorée du bistro et au mobilier, se fondent dans le design de Philippe Starck. L'hôtel présente la gamme complète indispensable pour un séjour exceptionnel : une scène, un spa, une boutique, un bar-piscine et de superbes pièces pour les manifestations.

Ya la entrada parece una catedral Alan Faena, fundador de la marca Via Vai, creó a partir de un antiguo granero un universo estilístico sin precedentes en Buenos Aires. El diseño de Philippe Starck introduce elementos de la Belle Époque, claramente visibles en el mobiliario y la pompa blanca-dorada de los bistrós. El hotel dispone de un área completa para una vida de súper lujo: Teatro, spa, boutique, piscina-bar y elegantes salones para la celebración de eventos.

Già l'ingresso ha l'aspetto maestoso di una cattedrale. Alan Faena, fondatore della griffe Via Vai, ha trasformato un vecchio granaio in un universo all'insegna del lifestyle che a tutt'ora non ha pari a Buenos Aires. Il design firmato Philippe Starck ben si mescola con un tocco di belle époque, evidente soprattutto nello sfarzo bianco-oro del bistrò e del mobilio. L'hotel rappresenta un microcosmo in cui si concretizza un concetto di vita in grande stile, con un repertorio completo di palcoscenico, Spa, boutique, pool bar ed eleganti sale eventi.

A regal reception—the central aisle of the brick-built building rises to a height of ten meters.

Ein großer Empfang – das 10 Meter hohe Mittelschiff des Backsteingebäudes.

Un accueil grandiose – la nef centrale du bâtiment en briques affiche dix mètres de hauteur.

Una gran entrada – la nave central de 10 metros de altura del edificio de ladrillo.

Una grande reception ubicata nella "navata centrale" alta dieci metri dell'edificio in mattoni a vista.

Royal red and white dominates in over 100 rooms and suites.

Royales Rot-Weiß dominiert die über 100 Zimmer und Suiten.

Les couleurs royales rouge et blanc dominent les 100 chambres et suites.

Los regios colores blanco y rojo predominan en las 100 habitaciones y suites.

Rosso reale-bianco le note cromatiche predominanti nelle oltre 100 stanze e suite.

Four Seasons Hotel Buenos Aires

Buenos Aires, Argentina

Buenos Aires is affectionately known as the Paris of Latin America, a reputation that is reflected in the design of the Four Seasons Hotel. Built entirely in the style of an early 20th century French mansion, it blends in perfectly with the venerable façades that surround the hotel. This historical splendor is coupled with an atmosphere of unbridled luxury, including bathtubs made of pure marble and opulent furnishings. There are 138 rooms and 27 suites across twelve floors.

Man bezeichnet Buenos Aires gern als das Paris von Lateinamerika. Dergestalt zeigt sich auch das Four Seasons Hotel. Passend zu den alten Fassaden der Umgebung wurde es ganz und gar im französischen Stil des frühen 20. Jahrhunderts gestaltet. Zwar wirkt der dargebotene Prunk historisierend, doch die Bäder aus purem Marmor und die opulente Raumausstattung erzeugen ein Gefühl von wahrem Luxus. Über zwölf Stockwerke verteilen sich die 138 Zimmer und 27 Suiten.

On entend souvent dire que Buenos Aires est le Paris de l'Amérique latine. Le Four Seasons Hotel correspond à cette description. En harmonie avec les anciennes façades des alentours, il a été entièrement aménagé selon le style français du début du 20ème siècle. L'apparat représenté a certes un effet historisant, mais les salles de bain en marbre pur et l'équipement opulent des pièces procurent une sensation de luxe véritable. Les 138 chambres et les 27 suites sont réparties sur douze étages.

A Buenos Aires se le suele considerar el París de Latinoamérica. Así se muestra el hotel Four Seasons. En armonía con las antiguas fachadas de los alrededores, el hotel se diseñó totalmente al estilo francés de principios del siglo XX. Si bien es verdad que la citada suntuosidad le otorga un aire de pasado, los baños de mármol y la opulenta decoración crean un ambiente de verdadero lujo. En las doce plantas se distribuyen 138 habitaciones y 27 suites.

Buenos Aires viene definita spesso come la Parigi latinoamericana. E parigina è anche la veste in cui si presenta il Four Seasons Hotel, interamente realizzato nello stile francese d'inizio XX secolo, in linea con il contesto architettonico in cui è ubicato. E se il primo impatto è quello di un fasto un po' retrò, i bagni in marmo e lo stile opulento delle stanze trasmettono piuttosto una sensazione di lusso puro. Le 138 stanze e 27 suite sono distribuite su dodici piani.

Guests can enjoy all the trappings of a stately home in the Fours Seasons Hotel Buenos Aires.

Im Gestus eines herrschaftlichen Hauses empfängt das Fours Seasons in Buenos Aires seine Gäste.

Le Four Seasons accueille ses visiteurs à Buenos Aires tel une maison princière.

El hotel Four Seasons de Buenos Aires recibe a sus huéspedes al modo de una casa señorial.

Con l'eleganza e la signorilità che gli è propria, così il Four Seasons di Buenos Aires accoglie i suoi ospiti.

The historical design is particularly prominent in the high-ceilinged lobby.

Der historische Stil kommt in den hohen Räumen der Lobby besonders zur Geltung.

Le style historique est particulièrement bien mis en évidence dans les pièces hautes de plafond du lobby.

Ese estilo de épocas pasadas se pone especialmente de manifiesto en las estancias de techos altos del lobby.

Lo stile storico viene particolarmente valorizzato dagli alti soffitti della lobby.

Explora en Atacama

San Pedro, Chile

Clarity is key here, a recurring theme mirrored in everything from the architecture and interior design to the kitchen and restaurant. The hotel's low-set, elongated building has 50 rooms grouped around three inner courtyards. It is reminiscent of a ranch building, albeit a distinctly avant-garde one. Architect German del Sol, who drew inspiration from the Atacama desert in Northern Chile which is 8,000 feet above sea level, wants the hotel to be interpreted as an integral part of the surrounding scenery.

Klarheit lautet die Leitidee, dem sich das Konzept dieses Hotels verschrieben hat – die Architektur, das Interior-Design, die Küche der Restaurants. Die langgestreckten niedrigen Gebäude mit den 50 Gästezimmern, die sich um drei Innenhöfe gruppieren, erinnern an eine Ranch, wenn auch an eine ausgesprochen avantgardistische. Architekt German del Sol ließ sich von der auf 2400 Meter Höhe gelegenen Atacama Wüste im Norden Chiles inspirieren, will das Hotel als integralen Bestandteil der umgebenden Natur verstanden wissen.

La clarté, voilà l'idée directrice qui a prévalu dans le concept de cet hôtel : l'architecture, le design intérieur, la cuisine des restaurants. Avec leurs 50 chambres, les bâtiments peu élevés et allongés, groupés autour de trois cours intérieures, rappellent un ranch, mais un ranch très avant-gardiste. L'architecte German del Sol s'est inspiré du désert d'Atacama situé à 2400 mètres d'altitude au Nord du Chili et considère que l'hôtel fait partie intégrante de la nature environnante.

La claridad marca las directrices que se ha propuesto este hotel, tanto en la arquitectura, el diseño interior, como en la cocina de los restaurantes. Los bajos y extensos edificios con 50 habitaciones dispuestas alrededor de tres patios interiores recuerdan a un rancho, si bien de diseño vanguardista. El arquitecto German del Sol se inspiró en el desierto de Atacama situado a 2400 metros de altura en el norte de Chile con el deseo de que este hotel forme parte de su entorno natural.

Sobrietà è l'idea di fondo che sottende l'intera concezione dell'hotel, dalla struttura architettonica all'interior design nonché alla cucina del ristorante. Gli edifici bassi dalla forma allungata dotati di 50 camere degli ospiti distribuite attorno a tre cortili interni ricordano la struttura di un ranch, anche se in versione decisamente avanguardistica. Traendo ispirazione dal deserto di Atacama, a 2400 metri di altezza nel nord del Cile, l'architetto German del Sol ha concepito l'hotel come parte integrante della natura circostante.

The idea of simplicity, stripping things down to their bare essentials, is also mirrored in the interior design.

Die Idee von Einfachheit, auf das Notwendige reduziert, spiegelt sich auch im Innern wieder.

L'idée de la simplicité, réduite au maximum, se reflète également à l'intérieur.

La idea de la sencillez, reducida a lo esencial, se refleja también en el interior.

L'idea della semplicità, ridotta al puramente necessario, si riflette anche negli interni.

The masterful interplay of light and shadow echoes like a leitmotif through the entire hotel building.

Das virtuose Spiel mit Licht und Schatten zieht sich wie ein Leitmotiv durch den gesamten Hotelbau.

Tel un leitmotiv, le jeu virtuose de la lumière et de l'ombre se retrouve dans tous les bâtiments de l'hôtel.

Ese juego genial de luz y sombra sirve como leitmotiv que impregna todo el hotel.

I giochi di luce ed ombre, magistralmente riprodotti, ricorrono come un leitmotiv nell'intera struttura.

Architecture in harmony with nature: colors and shapes reflect the surrounding nature.

Architektur im Einklang mit der Natur: Farben und Formen nehmen die umgebende Natur auf.

En harmonie avec la nature : les couleurs et les formes de l'architecture reprennent celles de la nature environnante.

La arquitectura en perfecta armonía con la naturaleza: los colores y las formas están integradas en el entorno natural.

Architettura in simbiosi con la natura: colori e forme sembrano assorbire la natura circostante.

Index

Canada

Princess Royal Isl.

King Pacific Lodge, A Rosewood Resort
Princess Royal Island, British Columbia V7M 3G8, Canada
T +1 604 987 5452, F +1 604 987 5472
www.kingpacificlodge.com

17 accommodations. Dining room, Great Room with rock-clad fireplace, fireside library. High-powered telescope, sun deck, and large open deck for open-air dining. Guided wildlife viewing, ocean fishing, fly fishing, kayaking, heli skiing, and hiking. Nestled in the Great Bear Rainforest on the north coast of British Columbia, 56 miles south of Prince Rupert. Access by privately chartered plane from Vancouver to Bella Bella on the North Coast. From there, transfer to the lodge by floatplane.

Vancouver

Opus
322 Davie Street, Vancouver, British Columbia V6B 5Z6, Canada
T +1 604 642 6787, F +1 604 642 6780
www.opushotel.com

96 guest rooms and suites. Restaurant and bar, meeting and catering services for up to 50 guests. Fitness room open 24 hours, complimentary hotel car service to all downtown locations. Situated in the Yaletown district of downtown Vancouver, within walking distance of the city's financial and retail centers.

Hawaii

Ka'upulehu-Kona

Four Seasons Resort Hualalai
100 Ka'upulehu Drive, Ka'upulehu-Kona, Hawaii 96740, USA
T +1 808 325 8000, F +1 808 325 8053
www.fourseasons.com

243 bungalow-style guest rooms, including 31 suites. Some of the lower-level rooms and suites offer outdoor gardens and lava rock showers. One Presidential Villa. Restaurant with ocean view. 24-hour in-room dining. Hualalai Sports Club and Spa with lap pool, whirlpools, saunas, steam rooms and cold plunges in tropical gardens. Pool, eight tennis courts, 18-hole Jack-Nicklaus Hualalai Golf Course. Meeting facilities. Ten-minute drive from Kona International Airport.

Honolulu

Sheraton Moana Surfrider
2365 Kalakaua Avenue, Honolulu, Hawaii 96815, USA
T +1 808 922 3111, F +1 808 924 4799
www.moana-surfrider.com

793 rooms, including 46 suites. Three restaurants and lounges, snack bar and grill. Fitness center, tennis, swimming pool. Located in the heart of Waikiki Beach, nine miles from Honolulu International Airport.

Wyoming

Jackson Hole

Amangani
1535 North East Butte Road, Jackson Hole, Wyoming 83001, USA
T +1 877 734 7333, F +1 307 734 7332
www.amanresorts.com

29 suites, six Deluxe Suites, four Amangani Suites and the Grand Teton Suite, all featuring fireplaces. The Grill dining room with fireplace, bar with adjacent terrace, lounge. Library. Health center, gym, 115-feet heated outdoor swimming pool and whirlpool. 20 minutes from Jackson Hole Airport by complimentary transfer. Less than 65 miles from Yellowstone National Park.

California

San Francisco

Four Seasons Hotel San Francisco
757 Market Street, San Francisco, California 94103, USA
T +1 415 633 3000, F +1 415 633 3001
www.fourseasons.com

277 guest rooms, including 46 suites. Restaurant, lounge and bar. Pool, spa and fitness facilities, sauna/steam rooms. Located in the Yerba Buena cultural district, two blocks from Union Square, the Financial District, the Moscone Convention Center and the Museum of Modern Art.

Big Sur

Post Ranch Inn
Highway 1, PO Box 219, Big Sur, California 93920, USA
T +1 831 667 2200, F +1 831 667 2824
www.postranchinn.com

30 non-smoking rooms, restaurant Sierra Mar overlooking the Ocean. Spa, massages, aromatherapy, crystal and gemstone treatment, shamanic consultation session. 30 minutes south of Carmel and two hours south of San José International Airport.

Beverly Hills

Beverly Hills Hotel
9641 Sunset Boulevard, Beverly Hills, California 90210, USA
T +1 310 276 2251, F +1 310 887 2887
www.thebeverlyhillshotel.com

204 guest rooms and suites, including 21 one-of-a-kind bungalows. Restaurant and bar. Three ballrooms, business services. 20 minutes from Los Angeles International Airport.

Beverly Hills

Raffles L'Ermitage Beverly Hills
9291 Burton Way, Beverly Hills, California 90210, USA
T +1 310 278 3344, F +1 310 278 8247
www.lermitagehotel.com

124 guest rooms and suites. Restaurant and bar. Amrita Spa and Amrita Spa cuisine, meeting room. Outside swimming pool with poolside cabanas. Located in the center of Beverly Hills.

Dana Point

The Ritz-Carlton, Laguna Niguel
1 Ritz-Carlton Drive, Dana Point, California 92629, USA
T +1 949 240 2000, F +1 949 240 0829
www.ritzcarlton.com

393 rooms, including 30 suites and 38 Ritz-Carlton Club Level rooms. Restaurant 162' with ocean view nestled 162 feet above the ocean, club grill and bar, pool bar. Spa, tennis, swimming, surfing, boogie boarding, sailing, kayaking, sport fishing, and whale watching. 19 meeting rooms, pool terraces, oceanfront lawns. Two miles of sandy beach. 25 miles from John Wayne International Airport, 65 miles from Los Angeles International Airport.

Palm Springs

The Parker Palm Springs
4200 East Palm Canyon Drive, Palm Springs, California 92264, USA
T +1 760 770 5000, F +1 760 324 2188
www.theparkerpalmsprings.com

131 rooms and 13 villas. Two restaurants and bar, two indoor and two outdoor pools. Spa, tennis, five meeting rooms. Palm Springs Yacht Club. Ten-minute drive from Palm Springs National Airport.

Nevada

Las Vegas

THEhotel at Mandalay Bay
3950 Las Vegas Boulevard South, Las Vegas, Nevada 89119, USA
T +1 877 632 7800
www.thehotelatmandalaybay.com

117 suites with separate living and sleeping areas, 21 restaurants, 24-hour cafe, coffee bar, relaxing lounge, and restaurant and lounge atop the hotel. Business Suites. Bathhouse spa with pools of varying temperatures, exotic baths, and flowing waterfall. Gym with personal trainers. Meeting facilities and convention center.

Arizona

Scottsdale

Sanctuary on Camelback Mountain
5700 East McDonald Drive, Scottsdale, Arizona 85253, USA
T +1 480 948 2100
www.sanctuaryoncamelback.com

98 luxurious mountain and spa casitas. Views ballroom, accommodating 200 guests for banquet seating, spa, restaurant. Located eight miles north of Phoenix's Sky Harbor International Airport and less than five minutes from downtown Scottsdale.

Scottsdale

Hyatt Regency Scottsdale Resort and Spa at Gainey Ranch
7500 East Doubletree Ranch Road, Scottsdale, Arizona 85258, USA
T +1 480 444 1234, F +1 480 483 5550
www.scottsdale.hyatt.com

490 rooms, including 25 suites and eight casitas. Four restaurants, Water Garden, and two bars. Spa at Gainey Ranch. Ten swimming pools, two ballrooms, 29 meeting rooms, business center. Complimentary shopping shuttle. 20 minutes from Sky Harbor International Airport.

Florida

Miami Beach

The Ritz-Carlton, South Beach
1 Lincoln Road, Miami Beach, Florida 33139, USA
T +1 786 276 4000, F +1 786 276 4100
www.ritzcarlton.com

376 guest rooms, including 54 poolside lanai rooms, 40 suites, 67 Ritz-Carlton Club Level rooms and suites and 1 Ritz-Carlton Suite. Three restaurants, beach club. Spa with 14 treatment rooms, pool. Ballroom, ten meeting rooms. Original art collection featuring established and emerging artists. Located directly on the beach.

Miami Beach

The Raleigh Hotel
1775 Collins Avenue, Miami Beach, Florida 33139, USA
T +1 305 534 6300, F +1305 538 8140
www.raleighhotel.com

104 rooms and suites, oceanfront three-bedrooms, 6,000-square feet penthouse. Restaurant and bar, meeting and conference facilities, swimming pool with cascading waterfall, in-room and poolside spa, massage services. Situated in the Art Deco District, some steps to restaurants, shopping and beach.

Miami Beach

The Setai
2001 Collins Avenue, Miami Beach, Florida 33139, USA
T +1 305 520 6000, F +1 305 520 6600
www.setai.com

125 suites with one, two, and three bedrooms, 10000-square feet penthouse with rooftop pool. Restaurant, lounge bar and beach bar. Three beachfront pools. Spa with ocean view. Fitness center with personal trainers, yoga, tai chi. Water sports, golf, tennis. Located on the beach of South Beach.

Illinois

Chicago

Park Hyatt Chicago
800 North Michigan Avenue, Chicago, Illinois 60611, USA
T +1 312 335 1234, F +1 312 239 4000
www.hyatt.com

202 guest rooms, including nine suites. 162 non-smoking rooms available. Restaurant and bar. Spa, 25-yard pool, meeting rooms. Located within walking distance of the city's premiere cultural centers, architecture, and upscale retailers.

Chicago

The Peninsula Chicago
108 East Superior, Chicago, Illinois 60611, USA
T +1 312 337 2888, F +1 312 751 2888
www.chicago.peninsula.com

339 guest rooms and suites, four restaurants, and bar. 14,000-square foot Peninsula Spa on the top two floors with natural light, half-olympic-length indoor swimming pool, outdoor sundeck with health-conscious spa cuisine. Fitness center, ballroom and meeting facilities.

Chicago

Sofitel Chicago Watertower
20 East Chestnut Street, Chicago, Illinois 60611, USA
T +1 312 324 4000, F +1 312 324 4026
www.sofitel.com

415 rooms, including 33 suites, non-smoking floors. Restaurant and bar, nine meeting rooms, ballroom, fitness center, massage. Views of the Michigan Lake. Located in downtown Chicago, close to the famous Magnificent Mile.

Massachusetts

Boston

Fifteen Beacon
15 Beacon Street, Boston, Massachusetts 02108, USA
T +1 617 670 1500, F +1 617 670 2525
www.xvbeacon.com

60 rooms, studios, and suites, featuring working gas fireplaces and whirlpool tubs. Wine Cellar. Complimentary in-town chauffeured sedan service. Located atop historic Beacon Hill.

New York

New York

Four Seasons Hotel New York
57 East 57th Street, New York, New York 10022, USA
T +1 212 758 5700, F +1 212 758 5711
www.fourseasons.com

364 rooms, some with furnished terraces, including 61 suites. Restaurant L'Atelier de Joel Robuchon, 57 Restaurant and TY Lounge. Spa with whirlpool, sauna, and steam room. In Manhattan's premier business and shopping district. 30 minutes from LaGuardia Airport.

New York

Mandarin Oriental, New York
80 Columbus Circle at 60th Street, New York, New York 10023, USA
T +1 212 805 8800, F +1 212 805 8888
www.mandarinoriental.com

202 rooms and 46 suites on floors 35 to 54 with floor-to-ceiling views. Restaurant and lobby lounge on the 35th floor. 14500-square feet spa, gym, swimming pool, fitness center. Located on the top of the Time Warner Center at the Southwest tip of Central Park, a ten-minute walk from Fifth Avenue.

New York

Hotel (The Mercer)
147 Mercer Street, New York, New York 10012, USA
T +1 212 966 6060, F +1 212 965 3838
www.mercerhotel.com

75 loft-like rooms and suites on six floors. Restaurant on two floors, comprising a 40-seats street-level café adjacent to the hotel lobby. Private trainers, yoga, massage therapists. Located in Soho.

New York

Plaza Athénée
37 East 64th Street, New York, New York 10021, USA
T +1 212 734 9100, F +1 212 772 0958
www.plaza-athenee.com

149 rooms on 17 floors including 35 suites with dining rooms and/or indoor atriums and outdoor balconies. Restaurant Arabelle with modern French cuisine, Bar Seine. Banquet and meeting facilities. Nestled on the East Side of Manhattan, some steps from Madison Avenue and Central Park.

New York

The Lowell
28 East 63rd Street, New York, New York 10021, USA
T +1 212 838 1400, F +1 212 319 4230
www.lowellhotel.com

47 individually decorated suites and 23 deluxe rooms. Many suites with fireplaces and terraces. Two restaurants, fitness center with Health Snack Station. Located on a quiet street between Madison Avenue and Park Avenue, in the heart of the exclusive and fashionable Upper East Side.

Bahamas

Emerald Bay

Four Seasons Resort Great Exuma
Emerald Bay, Great Exuma, Bahamas
T +1 242 336 6800, F +1 242 336 6801
www.emeraldbayresort.com

183 guest rooms and suites with terrace or balcony, two Royal Beachfront Villas, each with private pool. Restaurant, grill, and lounge. Full-service spa, spa garden, health club, steam massage. 18-hole championship golf course, six tennis courts, water sports. Supervised activities for children and children's pool. 15 minutes from Exuma International Airport.

Paradise Island

One&Only Ocean Club
Paradise Island, Bahamas
T +1 242 954 809 2150, F +1 242 363 2424
www.oneandonlyresorts.com

106 rooms, including 14 suites nestled in two wings of different small buildings, garden cottages and villas. Two restaurants, pool terrace cafe, gourmet in-room dining. Full-service spa, two pools. 18-hole championship golf course, six tennis courts, complimentary non-motorized water sports. Two meeting rooms for small meetings. Located a short ride from Nassau International Airport.

Caribbean

Anguilla

St. Regis Temenos Villas
Temenos, Long Bay, Anguilla, British West Indies
T +1 264 222 9000, F +1 264 498 9050
www.starwoodhotels.com

Three two-story villas overlooking the beach of Long Bay, with marble indoor and outdoor bathrooms. Infinity-edge pool with poolside jacuzzi. Private terraces and outdoor dining pavilion. Spa. Snorkeling, fishing, sailing, scuba diving, tennis, yoga. Flight into Anguilla's Wallblake Airport from San Juan in one hour, from Antigua in 45 minutes, or from St. Maarten in seven minutes.

Antigua

Carlisle Bay
Old Road, St. Mary's, Antigua, British West Indies
T +1 268 484 0000, F +1 268 484 0001
www.carlisle-bay.com

80 suites, two restaurants, three bars. Spa with six treatment rooms, sauna, plunge pools, gym, yoga, personal trainers, water sports, tennis. 30 minutes from Antigua International Airport.

Virgin Gorda

Little Dix Bay, A Rosewood Resort
Virgin Gorda, British Virgin Islands
T +1 284 495 5555, F +1 284 495 5661
www.littledixbay.com

100 guest rooms, including eight Junior Suites, four one-bedroom suites, and two private villas. Three restaurants, private beach dinners. Spa, water sports, water taxi to one of eleven secluded beaches nearby. Sailing, kayaking, diving, snorkeling, and deep sea fishing. Five minutes from Virgin Gorda Airport.

Mustique

Cotton House
St. Vincent, Mustique, The Grenadines
T +1 784 456 4777, F +1 784 456 5887
www.cottonhouse.net

19 suites and rooms in cottages, some with private plunge pools. Cotton Hill Residence with private pool. Beach restaurant, gastronomic restaurant, beach bars. Pool and spa. 45 minutes from Barbados International Airport.

St. Barthélemy

Le Sereno
St. Barthélemy, French West Indies
T +1 590 590 29 83 00
www.lesereno.com

37 suites and villas. Gourmet restaurant, bar and lounge. Beachfront freshwater swimming pool, spa, fitness center. Private airport transportation. Resort located in the heart of the French West Indies, 16 miles southeast of St. Maarten.

St. Martin

La Samanna
St. Martin, French West Indies
T +1 590 590 87 64 00, F +1 590 590 87 87 86
www.lasamanna.com

81 air conditioned guest rooms, suites, and villas. Restaurant, Bar de Champagne, beach bar and wine cellar. Freshwater swimming pool, spa offering a wide range of massages and spa treatments, three tennis courts, water sports. Daily direct flights from the US, France, and the Netherlands. Ten-minute drive from the airport.

St. Lucia

Anse Chastanet
Soufriere, St. Lucia, British West Indies
T +1 758 459 7000, F +1 758 459 7700
www.ansechastanet.com

49 individually designed rooms in different buildings. Restaurant with terrace, overlooking the coast. Spa, yoga, snorkeling, diving, windsurfing, ocean kayaking, sunfish sailing. Jade Mountain: resort within a resort. Located on the southwest coast, 1,5 hours from the airport by car.

Mexico

Mexico City

Camino Real México
Mariano Escobedo 700, Mexico City 11590, Mexico
T +52 55 5263 8888, F +52 55 5531 0839
www.caminoreal.com

712 rooms and suites. Seven restaurants and bars. Two swimming pools, gym. 20 meeting rooms. Eight acres of gardens. Located in the exclusive financial and commercial zone of Polanco, close to the Bosque de Chapultepec and the Museum of Modern Art.

Mexico City

Sheraton Centro Histórico
Avenida Juarez 70, Mexico City 06010, Mexico
T +52 55 5130 5300, F +52 55 5130 5255
www.sheratonmexico.com

457 guest rooms and suites. Two restaurants, bar, and lounge. 14 meeting rooms, fitness center, business center. 15 minutes from the International Airport.

Puerto Vallarta

Hotelito Desconocido
Aldanaca 178 4A, Col. Versalles, Puerto Vallarta, Jalisco 48310, Mexico
T +52 322 281 4010, F +52 322 281 4130
www.hotelito.com

12 buildings on stilts and 12 beach bungalows. Two restaurants, bar. Pool, "primitive-luxury spa" offering a range of massages and treatments. Natural jacuzzi and steam bath, yoga. Secluded sand beach. Horse riding. No electricity and no phone. 1,5-hour drive south of Puerto Vallarta.

Riviera Maya

Esencia
Playa Xpu-Ha, Riviera Maya, Mexico
T +1 877 528 3490, F +52 984 873 4835
www.hotelesencia.com

29 accommodations in different suites and cottages, featuring furnishings crafted from native woods, terraces, plunge pools, and private solariums. Restaurant Sal y Fuego featuring fresh seafood. Organic spa specialized in fito-therapy. Yoga, couples'spa suites, and jacuzzis. 40 miles from Cancun Airport.

Riviera Maya

Ikal del Mar
Quintana Roo, Playa Xcalacoco, Riviera Maya 77710, Mexico
T +52 984 877 3000, F +52 984 877 3009
www.ikaldelmar.com

30 bohios with private terraces, gardens, and plunge pools, one two-story Presidential Villa. Restaurant and beach bar. Mayan spa with temascal, direct beach access. 40 minutes from Cancun International Airport.

Yucatán

Hacienda Temozón
KM 182 Carretera Merida-Uxmal, Temozon Sur, Yucatán 97825, Mexico
T +52 999 923 8089, F +52 999 923 7963
www.starwood.com

28 guest rooms and suites, featuring terraces. Restaurant with view over the gardens. Spa, outdoor pool. Three meeting rooms. 164 miles from Merida Airport.

Belize

Placencia

Turtle Inn
Placencia, Belize
T +1 501 824 4912
www.turtleinn.com

Eight two-bedroom and two-bathroom villas. 17 cottages. Restaurant and two bars. Spa and pool. Complimentary kayaks and bicycles available. Located outside the town of San Ignacio.

Brazil

São Paulo

Emiliano
Rua Oscar Freire 384, 01426-000 São Paulo, Brazil
T +55 11 3069 4369
www.emiliano.com.br

57 rooms. Restaurant and lobby bar. Spa, steam room, sauna, gym. Business center. Heli pad. Located right in the center of São Paulo.

São Paulo

Fasano
Rua Vittório Fasano 88, 01414-020 São Paulo, Brazil
T +55 11 3896 4077
www.fasano.com.br

60 rooms and suites. Two restaurants, one of them the Fasano Restaurant. Baretto jazz bar and lobby bar. Business center. Plunge pool sanctuary with sauna, steam room, and views of the skyscrapered horizon on 21st floor. Located in between Paulista avenue and Faria Lima, nearby a trendy shopping area. Less than one mile from downtown, six miles from São Paulo Cogonhas Airport.

Argentina

Buenos Aires

Faena Hotel + Universe
445 Martha Salotti, C1107CMB Buenos Aires, Argentina
T +54 11 4010 9000, F +54 11 4010 9001
www.faenahotelanduniverse.com

105 rooms and suites. Restaurant, bistro, spa, and pool bar. Business center. Outside swimming pool, library lounge. Experienced hosts accompany guests to tango, polo and horseracing events. Located in the heart of the El Porteno Art District in Puerto Madero, Buenos Aires.

Buenos Aires

Four Seasons Buenos Aires
Posadas 1086/88, C1011ABB Buenos Aires, Argentina
T +54 11 4321 1200, F +54 11 4321 1201
www.fourseasons.com

138 rooms and 27 suites, restaurant, and lounge. Library, outdoor heated pool, meeting rooms. Adjacent to the city's exclusive La Recoleta District. 40-minute drive from Ezeiza International Airport.

Chile

San Pedro

Explora en Atacama
San Pedro, Atacama, Chile
T +56 2 206 6060, F +56 2 228 4655
www.explora.com

50 rooms, restaurant and bar. Four outdoor pools, sauna, jacuzzi. Art gallery featuring Atacama Indian artcrafts, meeting room. Located outside San Pedro de Atacama. 2,5-hour flight from Santiago de Chile International Airport to Calama. One-hour van ride pick-up service from and to Calama.

Photo Credits

Roland Bauer	The Ritz-Carlton, South Beach	76, 77, 79
	Four Seasons Resort Great Exuma	126
	One&Only Ocean Club	130
Katharina Feuer	Faena Hotel + Universe	204, 205, 207
	Four Seasons Buenos Aires	208, 210, 211
Michelle Galindo	The Setai	84
	Sofitel Chicago Watertower	96
Gavin Jackson	Four Seasons Hotel San Francisco	34
	Post Ranch Inn	6, 38
	The Ritz-Carlton, Laguna Niguel	52
	The Parker Palm Springs	56
	Four Seasons Hotel New York	104
	Mandarin Oriental, New York	110, 111, 113
	Hotel (The Mercer)	9, 114-117
	Plaza Athénée	118
	Emiliano	194
	Fasano	200
Nikolas Koenig	Faena Hotel + Universe	206
Karin Kohlberg	The Lowell	122-124
Martin Nicholas Kunz	Raffles L'Ermitage Beverly Hills	48
	Sanctuary on Camelback Mountain	13, 66
	Hyatt Regency Scottsdale Resort and Spa at Gainey Ranch	72-75
	The Setai	85, 87
	Park Hyatt Chicago	88-91
	Sofitel Chicago Watertower	96, 98, 99
	Anse Chastanet	160, 163
	Camino Real México	164, 165, 167
	Sheraton Centro Histórico	168
	Esencia	176
	Ikal del Mar	180
Jean-Philippe Piter	Le Sereno	150

Other photos courtesy

Accor Hotels & Resorts	Sofitel Chicago Watertower	10, 97
Amanresorts	Amangani	30
André Balazs Properties	Hotel (The Mercer)	117
Anse Chastanet	Anse Chastanet	161, 162
Beverly Hills Hotel	Beverly Hills Hotel	44
Camino Real México	Camino Real México	164, 166
Carlisle Bay	Carlisle Bay	138
Explora	Explora en Atacama	212
Faena Hotel + Universe	Faena Hotel + Universe	204, 207
Fifteen Beacon	Fifteen Beacon	100
Four Seasons Hotels & Resorts	Four Seasons Resort Hualalai	22
	Four Seasons Buenos Aires	209
Francis Ford Coppola's Blancaneaux Resorts	Turtle Inn	190
GHM Hotels & Resorts	The Setai	84, 86
gla Hotels	Cotton House	146
Hotelito Desconocido	Hotelito Desconocido	172
Hyatt Hotels & Resorts	Hyatt Regency Scottsdale Resort and Spa at Gainey Ranch	75
	Park Hyatt Chicago	88
Mandarin Oriental Hotel Group	Mandarin Oriental, New York	Backcover, 112, 113
Opus	Opus	18
Orient-Express Hotels	La Samanna	156
Peninsula Hotels	The Peninsula Chicago	92
Rosewood Hotels & Resorts	King Pacific Lodge, A Rosewood Resort	14
	Little Dix Bay, A Rosewood Resort	142
Starwood Hotels & Resorts	Sheraton Moana Surfrider	26
	St. Regis Temenos Villas	134
	Hacienda Temozón	186
The Lowell	The Lowell	122, 125
The Raleigh Hotel	The Raleigh Hotel	80
The Ritz-Carlton Hotel Company	The Ritz-Carlton, South Beach	78, 79
THEhotel at Mandalay Bay	THEhotel at Mandalay Bay	Cover, 5, 62

Editors	Martin Nicholas Kunz, Patrice Farameh, Patricia Massó
Editorial Coordination	Rosina Geiger, Hanna Martin
Introduction	Patrice Farameh
Hotel Texts by	Patrice Farameh, Katharina Feuer, Bärbel Holzberg, Martin Nicholas Kunz, Heinfried Tacke
Layout & Prepress	Martin Nicholas Kunz
Imaging	Jan Hausberg
German Translation by	Carolin Schöngarth
Other Translations by	Artes Translations, Dr. Suzanne Kirkbright
English	Dr. Suzanne Kirkbright
French	Céline Verschelde, Brigitte Villaumié
Spanish	Alvira Gamboa, Carmen de Miguel
Italian	Paola Lonardi, Maria-Letizia Haas

Editorial project by fusion publishing gmbh, stuttgart . los angeles
www.fusion-publishing.com

Published by teNeues Publishing Group

teNeues Verlag GmbH + Co. KG
Am Selder 37, 47906 Kempen, Germany
Tel.: 0049-(0)2152-916-0, Fax: 0049-(0)2152-916-111

teNeues International Sales Division
Speditionstraße 17, 40221 Düsseldorf, Germany
Tel.: 0049-(0)211-994597-0, Fax: 0049-(0)211-994597-40

teNeues Publishing Company
16 West 22nd Street, New York, NY 10010, USA
Tel.: 001-212-627-9090, Fax: 001-212-627-9511

teNeues Publishing UK Ltd.
P.O. Box 402, West Byfleet, KT14 7ZF, Great Britain
Tel.: 0044-1932-403509, Fax: 0044-1932-403514

teNeues France S.A.R.L.
4, rue de Valence, 75005 Paris, France
Tel.: 0033-1-55766205, Fax: 0033-1-55766419

teNeues Iberica S.L.
c/Velázquez, 57 6.° izda., 28001 Madrid, Spain
Tel.: 0034-657-132133

teNeues Representative Office Italy
Via San Vittore 36/1, 20133 Milan, Italy
Tel.: 0039-(0)347-7640551

www.teneues.com

© 2006 teNeues Verlag GmbH + Co. KG, Kempen

ISBN-10: 3-8327-9142-6
ISBN-13: 978-3-8327-9142-1

Printed in Italy

Bibliographic information published by Die Deutsche Bibliothek.
Die Deutsche Bibliothek lists this publication in the Deutsche Nationalbibliografie; detailed bibliographic data is available in the Internet at http://dnb.ddb.de.